D1058836

HEIDEGGER'S SILENCE

OTHER BOOKS BY BEREL LANG

Art and Inquiry
The Human Bestiary
Faces, and Other Ironies of Writing and Reading
Philosophy and the Art of Writing
Act and Idea in the Nazi Genocide
*The Anatomy of Philosophical Style: Literary Philosophy
   and the Philosophy of Literature*
Writing and the Moral Self
Mind's Bodies: Thought in the Act

EDITED VOLUMES

Marxism and Art: Writing in Aesthetics and Criticism
The Concept of Style
Philosophical Style: An Anthology about the Writing and Reading of Philosophy
Philosophy and the Holocaust
The Philosopher in the Community: Essays in Memory of Bertram Morris
The Death of Art
Writing and the Holocaust

Heidegger's SILENCE

BEREL LANG

CORNELL UNIVERSITY PRESS

ITHACA AND LONDON

Copyright © 1996 by Cornell University

All rights reserved. Except for brief quotations in a review, this book, or parts thereof, must not be reproduced in any form without permission in writing from the publisher. For information, address Cornell University Press, Sage House, 512 East State Street, Ithaca, New York 14850.

First published 1996 by Cornell University Press.

Printed in the United States of America

♾ The paper in this book meets the minimum requirements of the American National Standard for Information Sciences—Permanence of Paper for Printed Library Materials, ANSI Z39.48-1984.

Library of Congress Cataloging-in-Publication Data

Lang, Berel,
     Heidegger's silence / Berel Lang.
        p. cm.
     Includes bibliographical references and index.
     ISBN 0-8014-3310-X (cloth : alk. paper)
        1. Heidegger, Martin, 1889-1976—Views on Jews.   2. Antisemitism—
Germany—History—20th century.   I. Title.
B3279.H49L36   1996
193—dc20   96-16193

LIBRARY
ALMA COLLEGE
ALMA, MICHIGAN

In grateful memory

ROBERT S. BRUMBAUGH

ALBERT HOFSTADTER

NATHAN ROTENSTREICH

Teachers, guides, friends

CONTENTS

PREFACE

B Y A ROUGH COUNT more has been written or at least published about Martin Heidegger than any other twentieth-century philosopher, and it seems almost certain that with the completion of the *Gesamtausgabe*—the edition of his collected works issued by Vittorio Klostermann, Frankfurt am Main (now in seventy-nine volumes and continuing)—his own published writings will also outnumber those of other twentieth-century and perhaps all modern philosophers. Given this large body of work and the diverse issues he addressed, it may seem captious to offer a book (even a short one) that associates Heidegger with an issue he did *not* write about—that takes as its subject his responsibility for the silence. But the thesis I mean to defend is just this: that the omission to be noted is notable; indeed, that Heidegger's silence on the Jewish Question is intended to speak—addressing and then denying this apparently narrow but, as becomes clear, broadly consequential issue in his thinking. Thus, his answer of silence to the Jewish Question becomes a reflection writ small (as small as absence, but not invisible) of the larger body of writing to which he openly set his name.

There is, I believe, nothing untoward (or for that matter novel) in putting such weight on silence, on what is *not* said or written. One need not have given in to fin-de-siècle melancholy or the new hyperconsciousness to be aware that absence or (in the author's voice) silence can be as deliberate and pointed as presence. Much less inventive than Sherlock Holmes, that premature postmodernist who had to *imagine* that the dog who did not bark would be a clue for recovering Silver Blaze, we find ourselves now almost incapable of *not* suspecting gaps in the many voices we listen to. And insofar as thinking, a condition for intention, is itself at issue, omissions or silence become still more significant. Admittedly, a sharp contrast appears in philosophy's history between an ideal of silence—the "inner conversation" that Plato identifies with thinking, or Aristotle's godlike aspiration for the philosopher toward "thinking about thinking"—and the bodily, often noisy representation of that ideal in philosophy's practice. But also in considering this representation, the willingness to write and read between the lines— to interpret absence—has been important not *in addition* to writing or reading the lines but as integral; it too can be intended, with its appearance epitomized in the act of denial, where the absence is all that is being asserted.

It is just such an articulate presence—an answer unspoken but an answer nonetheless—that I find in Heidegger's undoubted and oft-noted silence on the Jewish Question (a silence which extends, in a distinction to be elaborated, also to the "Jewish Question"). What, among alternative sources that include accident and indifference as well as purpose, is the significance of this silence? How, given the improbabilities uncovered in current theories of interpretation, can one speak with assurance about the "meaning" (or "the" meaning) of a textual moment (no matter how long) of silence? Can any causes or intentions motivating discourse be ruled out in the explanation of a particular absence that touch more than the will or mind of that one reader? These issues seem to me inescapable for the fullest or most overdetermined text; where what is under scrutiny is an oeuvre produced over a period of sixty years *and* in a life and practice closely interwoven with that writing—the background from which Heidegger now emerges—the difficulty in identifying patterns at all makes any pattern that does appear more markedly expressive. Heidegger's silence in answer to the Jewish Question seems to me to disclose just such a pattern—one which, despite that apparently parochial occasion, reverberates widely in his thinking.

What that "answer" asserts (more precisely, what the silence denies), how this denial is related to Heidegger's thought, and what this means for our retrospective view of Heidegger and of the Jewish Question—separately and joined—are the subjects of this book.

If OMISSIONS SPEAK, as I have suggested, the obligation of acknowledgment becomes ever more insistent. But I am glad to express my indebtedness to a number of people and sources. For their readings (sometimes, rereadings), for suggested revisions, for useful references, and for other combinations of criticism and encouragement, I thank Robert Bernasconi, Garry Brodsky, Joel Kraemer, Herbert Lindenberger, David Luban, Ricardo Nirenberg, Forrest Williams, and especially Felmon Davis, who willingly composed two drafts of his own comments. A reader for Cornell University Press made a number of pointed suggestions, and I hope I have taken the point. My wife, Helen S. Lang, here as always contributed more than generously a combination of professional acumen and personal support. I am grateful to the American Council of Learned Societies, the Center for Judaic Studies at the University of Pennsylvania, and the State University of New York for research grants that enabled me to work on the book.

The three of my onetime teachers—also guides and friends—to whom this volume is dedicated themselves held divergent views of both Heidegger and the Jewish Question; I could not then, even if there were a reason for wanting to, claim for them the view of those topics (or their relation) I offer here. But there also was—and remains—no doubt of their dedication to philosophy as practice or of their will for caring, as that remains the most difficult and rarely achieved of all philosophy's conditions. In them these impulses joined, ensuring that they would address ideas, like persons, as ends in themselves, and persons, however they came and wherever they stood, as bearers of an ideal of humanity. So in them there was hope.

B. L.

West Hartford, Connecticut
January 1996

HEIDEGGER'S   SILENCE

Every thinker thinks but a single thought.

—Martin Heidegger, *Nietzsche*

A lack of historical sense is the congenital defect of all philosophers.

—Friedrich Nietzsche, *Human All Too Human*

"I am good"; who else can say this than the good man himself, and who would be less willing to affirm it?

—Martin Heidegger, *Being and Time*

From the Jewish Question to the "Jewish Question": A History of Silence

An Obsolete Joke

An Englishman, a Frenchman, and a Jew were each asked to write an essay about elephants. The Englishman chose as his topic "Hunting Elephants in the Raj"; the Frenchman settled on "How Elephants Make Love"; the Jew wrote about "The Elephant and the Jewish Question."

T HE TITLE OF this chapter might well provoke an objection before the reader turned a page: Why, this late in the day, revisit the archaic formula of the Jewish Question, which on the rare occasions when we now encounter it typically comes framed by the quotation marks of obsolescence? Put quite simply, there *is* no longer a Jewish Question, at least as the phrase once brought to mind a single question about the Jews, evidently the one that mattered. To recall the Jewish Question as it flourished in the nineteenth century and the first half of the twentieth is to find a strong contrast between our present and that past, as the phrase surfaced earlier in a medley of linguistic and ideological appearances. It was the *Judenfrage* to which answers were sought by Bruno Bauer and Karl Marx, divided on one side, and Hermann

Cohen and Theodor Herzl, fixed in opposition on the other, but together agreeing at least on their common provocation. And then it was framed in the French of Bernard Lazare (later also of Sartre), the Hebrew of Ahad Ha'am, and the Russian (soon in Yiddish translation) of Tolstoy and Lenin, in the English of Justice Brandeis (and Henry Ford) and by numerous other writers in those and other languages: a common point of reference for Jewish and non-Jewish authors alike, used without prejudice (*this* far) by both "philo-" and "anti"semites.[1] The term was understood by anyone who thought about the Jews because there was a (that is, the) Jewish Question whose formulation was generally understood and accepted, whatever disagreements then followed: the question of how the Jews were to live among the nations—or, conversely, from the perspective of the nations, how *they* were to live with the Jews.

But the phrase and the Question itself have now lost their currency, with two principal reasons accounting for that displacement. The first explains the disappearance of the Jewish Question by announcing its resolution: the Jewish Question ceased to exist (so the contention) with the founding of the State of Israel in 1948. After that, Jews, wherever they lived and willingly or not, entered a relationship with a country that resembled other countries in political definition. Thus the most obvious source—or cause—of the Jewish Question disappeared, and so also the Question itself. There *was* a Jewish state; Jews living outside it would now be addressed in terms similar to those characterizing any people with historical ties to a nation other than the one they happened to inhabit. No longer must European or American or Asian governments face the issue of how to classify this oddly persistent— apparently inescapable—group of people who until then, although claiming to be related to each other by more than religious ties, had been unable, except by the vaguest gesture, to point to any such means of support. ("The homeland of the Jews," Schopenhauer had caustically noted, "is other Jews.") Governments take account of governments (when they listen to anyone at all). And so Jews around the world—Zionists, non-Zionists, and anti-Zionists alike—benefited from the fact of Israel's existence if only to the extent that they could stop hearing the Jewish Question (or asking it themselves). That most Jews chose not to "return" to Israel was incidental; Israel was the answer to the Jewish Question as a *question* even if for most Jews individually it was not the answer to how or where they should live, even if they felt so much at home wherever they were that these questions—like *the* Question—had never troubled or perhaps even occurred to them.

But the emergence of the State of Israel is only a partial explanation for the disappearance of the Jewish Question. It is one at any rate that hardly touched Martin Heidegger, the central figure in this discussion—and given the limits of the mind as it might consider the endless sweep and variations of geography, there was no special reason it should have. As it happened, Heidegger was notably attached to his own locales: to Messkirch, his birthplace; to Freiburg where he studied and then, after a brief interval away, returned to live and to work from 1928 until his death in 1976; to Todtnauberg, the site of his mountain cottage and retreat in the Schwarzwald. Since he found it possible to wait until 1962, when he was seventy-three years old, to venture on his first trip to Greece—for him the source of the Being (and language) of philosophy—it is not difficult to understand how the more remote land (and then state) of Israel might escape his imagination, let alone his thinking.

No like exemption holds, however, for Heidegger's reticence in respect to the second reason for the obsolescence of the Jewish Question, and it is to the combination of cause and effect expressing themselves in *this* source that I call attention in these pages. The occasion defining this reason occurred a short time before the declaration of Israel's independence; like the Jewish Question, it came to be named by having the definite article attached to what was previously only a common, not a proper noun. I refer, of course, to "the Holocaust,"[2] and the stop *it* put to the Jewish Question. For in the aftermath of the Nazi genocide against the Jews that "succeeded" in destroying two-thirds of the Jewish population of Europe, it became clear to almost everyone that to ask then how Jews might live among the nations must be at least a cause of embarrassment and with little additional conscience, a moral offense. And this for the obvious reason that the Nazis' answer to the

Question had disabled the Question itself. It was, after all, the Jewish Question to which the "Final Solution" was directed—*Frage* eliciting *Lösung*. And if it seems unfair to ascribe responsibility to a question for the aberrant answers given it, we understand that answers are not given unless the questions they address have indeed been asked.

As we look backward from this twofold perspective, furthermore, the genealogy of the Jewish Question—the sources of its history—appears no more mysterious than do the circumstances of its demise. It was the Enlightenment (or equally euphemistically from the viewpoint of Jewish history, the Emancipation) that opened the possibility that Jews would live among and not only beside the nations. And we, the inheritors of the Enlightenment, even at this distance still moved by its fraternal principles, look back now with alternating admiration and repugnance at the two very different sets of answers evoked by the Question. To be sure, nobody is now obliged to decide exactly what they would have chosen to forgo in the Enlightenment so as to avoid the particular Question the "Final Solution" could appear to answer. But it is enough that the likelihood of this connection casts its shadow: backward to the Jewish Question as it was first posed because of the extension in Europe of civil rights to those who had not had them; forward to its later appearances, in the aftermath of the Holocaust and now, in discussions like the present one, through the retrospective framework of quotation marks.[3]

My purpose in recalling the original Jewish Question here—as the "Jewish Question"—begins in an expansion of this Chapter's title to a thesis reflecting an unusual conjunction between the life of the mind and the body of history, which converge pointedly and ominously in the political persona and the philosophical work of Martin Heidegger, as *these* converged in the stormy course of his lifetime (so at least is my claim). It has sometimes been asserted that for philosophers, as for scientists or craftsmen or laborers, any apparent connections between the public or social self and their "workerly" accomplishment turn out in the end to be accidental; that those two sides of the individual appear and so must be judged independently. The evidence and arguments I gather here, however, claim for the figure at its center the contrary conclusion: that whatever the public and the professional works of Heidegger imply about the connection between those two expressive means for other philosophers, for him at least the connection between them is demonstrable. *And* furthermore, that one perspective, if not the only one, from which this conjunction can be observed, tested, and measured is precisely the relation—superficially tangential and muted, mingling absence and presence—between Heidegger and the Jewish Question.

The Jewish Question may seem too slight and parochial an issue to serve as a basis for assessing either the theoretical work or the political and moral history of a philosopher whom an informed part of the learned world has for more than sixty years held to be among its most notable figures.[4] But twentieth-century history forcibly brought the Jewish Question onto the world stage, if not for its final appearance, at least for a decisive one. And Heidegger's individual history, set in motion in the Swabian village of Messkirch in 1889, brought him face-to-face with the Question with such intensity that the silence in which the encounter concluded remains itself a graphic representation, at once encompassing his public and his professional works and (I argue here) demonstrating, at least in him and perhaps for others, the affinity between the two.

The summary conclusion to this sequence of claims takes the form of a thesis that posits a causal relation between the Jewish Question and the "Jewish Question" in Heidegger's thinking— more exactly, a relation between the *absence* of those two Questions from that thinking. Thus: For the influential thinker Martin Heidegger, there was no Jewish Question retrospectively, in the post-Holocaust era (to be known then as the "Jewish Question"). And the reason for this silence is that there was no Jewish Question for Heidegger when the Question did exist—that is, before the Holocaust. The reason for *that* silence is to be found, moreover, not in accidental features of Heidegger's personality or history, but in a deliberate—thoughtful—affirmation on his part. And last, for that affirmation in turn: we see a connection in Heidegger between the domains of the political and the philosophical, the public and the private, the professional and the occasional—connections that have often been denied by both his defenders and his critics (although not, it has to be said, by Heidegger himself) and that have been less strenuously but more generally questioned in reference to the relation between the lives and works of philosophers as such. That certain private dispositions or tastes of Heidegger expressed themselves apart from his thinking could hardly be doubted even by someone knowing no more about Heidegger's life than what Heidegger found pertinent in Aristotle's: "He was born; he worked; he died." It just happens that Heidegger's view of the Jewish Question is not—such at least is the argument presented here—a matter of private disposition or taste. Rather, that view, which concludes with a denial of the Question—silence—is reflectively articulated, *thought*; and the view emerges as reflective and thought, notwithstanding the fact that it sometimes expresses itself in the same forms that otherwise suggest mere prejudice or the influence of social or cultural tradition.

The possible confusion of the two appearances of the Jewish Question in this thesis (once as the "Jewish Question," once as the Jewish Question)[5] will, I hope, soon be clarified. Certainly the former appearance—the Jewish Question as past, framed by quotation marks—can be articulated in terms that are well known; these are the terms of Heidegger's post-Holocaust silence or, on the few occasions when he broke that silence, the combination of what he omitted to say and of what, in speaking, he encumbered with generalization and abstraction. The refuge, in sum, that he sought by avoiding the historical particular—especially, if not only, when that particular appeared as the Jew.

I elaborate this part of my thesis by reformulating familiar evidence: those few overt expressions of Heidegger's post-Holocaust response to the Holocaust that in effect underscore his more overt—louder—silence.[6] The conclusion this evidence points to is, by contrast, explicit and precise. Even after the Holocaust was over and its consequences were known—fully in the public domain—Heidegger, who had encountered face-to-face numerous manifestations of the Holocaust and heard about others of greater enormity, remained silent. There was for him no "Jewish Question," no issue of what it was that had happened to the Jews among the nations (within or at the hands of *his* nation), of why what happened to them happened or of how to assess that occurrence in moral or more general philosophical terms—or of what any of these implied for future conduct or thought (including his own). In the thirty post-Holocaust prolific years of his life, about these matters there was silence.

For many commentators, including some who find in Heidegger's writing during those last thirty years the most significant contributions of his eventual oeuvre, this silence remains more troubling than anything Heidegger did or said while the Nazis (and for a year he himself, as rector of the University of Freiburg) were in power. Even the defenses sometimes given of this silence—half-meant or fully meant—reflect the concession they ostensibly deny: tendentious and exhortative ("What if he *had* spoken out retrospectively against Auschwitz or against his own Nazi affiliations? What would this change in the assessment of his philosophical work, except perhaps to make it easier to ignore for those wishing to do so anyway?") or straightforwardly unverifiable and unverified ("His writing and lecturing, certainly after his yearlong misadventure as rector and arguably even before that were through and through oppositional, he was speaking out virtually all the time; to recognize this one has only to read him—and his silences—subtly, supplely, willingly rather than willfully").[7]

Well, for the second claim there is the test of reading itself; for the first, the more accessible measure of common sense. And prior to either of them remains the challenge posed by Heidegger's silence and his own few (and symptomatic) interruptions of it. I shall be suggesting that, viewed together, their challenge subverts the apologias offered for him that in effect deny that the silence was indeed silent, that by his very silence Heidegger was addressing the Holocaust directly, forthrightly.[8] Such apologias, it is obvious, would also preclude all explanation of origins: without silence, there could be no reason (and no interest in it) for explanations of why the silence occurred. But in respect to this too I shall be making exactly the opposite claim: that Heidegger's post-Holocaust silence mirrors—follows from—his silence before that. There was no "Jewish Question" after the Holocaust for Heidegger, in other words, not because of the Holocaust, not even (except at the psychological margins) in personal reaction or afterthought reflecting his own small role in it or as a continuing expression of his antisemitism, but because the Jewish Question had not existed for him before then either. It would have been openly factitious, in bad faith, for Heidegger to address in retrospect a question that he had denied or ignored earlier, when it *was* real. And whether or not this was the reason, he in fact made no such pretense. Thus the fulcrum of the thesis argued here is also the fulcrum of his position: there was no Jewish Question for Heidegger when the Jewish Question existed—and that is why there would be no "Jewish Question" for him later, after the Holocaust marked a stopping point in the Question's history.[9]

In this way my second, conceptually more basic concern reaches further back historically than the "Jewish Question," asking why, when there *was* a Jewish Question, it did not exist for Heidegger. The explanation I propose can also be anticipated at this point, insofar as it bears on Heidegger's subsequent silence—at the same time evoking the disputed question of the relation between Heidegger's politics and his "thinking." What concludes, then, with his silence on the apparently superficial, even parochial "Jewish Question" discloses its roots not in Heidegger's personal history or prejudices, not even in the dramatic historical background to his pronouncements during his official tenure from 21 April 1933 to 23 April 1934 as rector (for the last part of that tenure as Führer) of the University of Freiburg—but in his thinking. His denial of the Jewish Question, and then of the "Jewish Question," is thus not only an occasion or by-product but a representation of that thinking. What precluded acknowledgment of the Jewish Question for Heidegger (so the line of argument goes) was the at once metaphysically and historically efficacious role he ascribed to the concept of the "Volk"—and within that domain, the privileged position he assigned to the *German* Volk because of its supposed access to Being or being (as Sein or Dasein) and to Truth. Given his conception of the German Volk in its "essence" and history, there was, quite simply, no place for the Jews in Heidegger's thinking—not as a matter of prejudice (although this too was present), but as a matter of categories. In following the progression of Heidegger's thought to this conclusion, we learn as much as the evidence discloses not only about his relation to the Jews (by implication, to a central impulse of Nazi Germany, that is, its war against the Jews) but about the philosophical foundation on which his definition of that relation was based—and so also, at least in part, to his work and his standing as a thinker.

Both in tracing his initial rejection of the Jewish Question and in examining Heidegger's retrospective denial of the "Jewish Question," I shall be referring to what Heidegger did not say and to what he could have said as well as to what he did say—considering, that is, the issues he would have had to confront if the Jewish Question, early or late, *had* existed for him. The two topics initially distinguished—"Heidegger and the 'Jewish Question,'" and "Heidegger and the Jewish Question"—can, moreover, be represented quite impersonally and, up to a point, nonjudgmentally. Indeed, the twofold formulation itself may seem to beg a crucial methodological question: Suppose Heidegger did deny or choose to ignore or preferred silence on the "Jewish Question" or the Jewish Question or both—Well, what then? Surely there were also other questions and "questions" that he (like any other writer) failed to address; and surely no one can impose on authors or thinkers the character and order of questions they are required to consider. Interests or concerns do not appear on command: Why then point invidiously to a "Question"—or Question—that Heidegger happened or even chose not to ask?

But Heidegger cannot leave the room so easily; nobody could. For in the contexts of his own history and the broader history that was part of, neither the Jewish Question nor the "Jewish Question" was a neutral issue that he might, with equal warrant, elect to consider or not. Their historical and philosophical presence was, even without the weight that retrospection would add to them, too evident—too much present—to sanction an abstract freedom of choice that might, as he rendered them, result in omission or silence. This objection would hold even for someone who had lived a life in every respect identical to Heidegger's but without once uttering the word central to his conception of human activity (and his own): "thinking." *With* that commitment, although presumably not undertaking to think all that could be thought, does he not propose, even promise, to think, at the very least to admit as a subject for thought, whatever is undeniably present? It is this ground that impels the conclusion that for Heidegger to have inadvertently or thoughtlessly neglected either the Jewish Question or the "Jewish Question" is improbable to the point of impossibility. We recognize here a moment where not to have thought about something can only be understood as itself an expression of choice, the thoughtful decision not to think.

And to this conclusion can be joined yet another consideration that echoes alongside Heidegger's denial of the Jewish Question (whatever interpretation one proposes of that): the fact of his antisemitism. The causal importance of this additional reference should not be exaggerated: the main theses asserted here—that there was no "Jewish Question" for Heidegger, and that this came about because there had been for him no Jewish Question—would hold even if antisemitism had occupied no place in the conceptual or historical process that led up to them. Antisemitism is thus not a necessary element in Heidegger's rejection of the "Jewish Question" or the Jewish Question (indeed, I shall be relating Heidegger's denial of them to his attitude first toward the Germans and only then toward the Jews). But if, on independent grounds, evidence *also* appears of his antisemitism, this would intensify an already consistent line of philosophical argument. For there would then be a basis in experience (more precisely, in psychology) to underscore the denial of the two Questions—thus also reinforcing the link asserted between his public life and his thought. If the latter relation does not amount to a necessary connection, it emerges (so the argument will claim) as more than an incidental or chance occurrence.

There is, I believe, sufficient evidence of the relation between Heidegger's rejection of both the Jewish Question and the "Jewish Question" and his philosophical work (however narrowly construed) even without the evidence of his antisemitism. With the addition of that evidence, Heidegger's silence on the Jewish Question (and then, through the Holocaust, on the "Jewish Question") takes the form of thinking unimpeded from the ground up. The lack of hindrance from the elements of his biography would by itself add a subsidizing weight to his "impersonal" thinking or speaking; with the addition of biographical—psychological, cultural, geographical—corroboration, his silence more clearly becomes denial, omission turns into assertion. By this, with this, he does indeed answer both the "Question" and the Question.

Thus too a filiation between "merely" psychological or personal disposition (the minimal grounds of antisemitism) and philosophical reflection announces itself in the Heidegger who appears now in retrospective view: the thinker seen whole, at that juncture of history and reflection that frames our present understanding of him. Exactly how the two factors of personal or commonplace disposition, on the one hand, and theoretical reflection, on the other, are systematically related in philosophy and philosophers is a more general and larger issue. Whatever view one holds of the question in this broader frame, however, the relationship it articulates in Heidegger is a point of origin for his views on both the Jewish Question and the "Jewish Question"—and so also for his refusal to recognize them *as* questions. Or so, at least, the following chapters propose.

The "Jewish Question" in Heidegger's Post-Holocaust

The two friends didn't meet again until after the war. One day Bultmann received a telephone call: "It's Martin here." He was so taken by surprise that he replied: "Forgive me, but which Martin is that?" Heidegger then explained the reason for his visit: "I should like to ask your pardon." The joyful reunion took place. . . . The day passed in a lively and animated exchange of ideas—just like the old days. . . . The past was forgotten. If he had once been drawn to National Socialism for good reasons, they had soon turned to disillusionment. Nothing more stood between us. As we were saying goodbye, I came back to what he had said on the telephone: "Now you'll have to write a retraction, like Augustine," I said, ". . . not least for the sake of the truth of your thought." Heidegger's face became a stony mask. He left without another word.

Recounted by Rudolf Bultmann to Hans Fischer-Barnicol

"Man speaks by being silent."

Martin Heidegger, What Is Called Thinking?

T HERE WAS, THEN—thus, the first part of my thesis—no post-Holocaust "Jewish Question" for Heidegger, nothing in or around the "Question" that he found worth talking about. The few intimations he gives of admitting that "Question" are oblique, subordinated to other, larger (in his view) concerns or concluding, even when directly provoked, in denial. Thus also the effect of these few words is to intensify rather than to overcome the silence. This absence cannot be attributed to a lack of information in or after 1945 or to the blurring effect of other events around him: the nature and extent of the Nazi genocide against the Jews were widely known (the Nuremberg trials ensured the availability of that information if by an unlikely chance other sources had failed). And Heidegger himself, with the leisure forced on him by his (as it turned out temporary) exclusion from the University of Freiburg as a result first of the university's own ruling and then of the French military government's verdict of 28 December 1946 ("Il est interdite à M. Heidegger d'enseigner et de participer à toute acti-vité de l'Université"],[1] if anything increased his remarkable pro-ductivity during those and later years. Even aside from this evidence, moreover, it seems impossible on prima facie grounds to find explanations for Heidegger's silence in ignorance or inadver-tence. Unaware he was not and could not have been—nor is he likely to have been too preoccupied; certainly it is difficult to iden-tify other topics that Heidegger intended to write about but found himself compelled to forgo because of only practical impediments.

Insofar, then, as the act of "thinking" is a keystone in Heideg-ger's own philosophical architectonic, there seems no alternative here to a conclusion of active rejection: Heidegger *refused* to think about the Holocaust, let alone to think it, with the refusal itself be-ing thought. (I echo here the theme of Hannah Arendt's tribute to Heidegger on his eightieth birthday: "Heidegger never thinks 'about' something; he thinks something.")[2] What this amounts to is an act of "postmeditation" at least equal in theoretical and moral weight to what premeditation adds to other evidence of agency. We are obliged, I believe, to speak further here of weight added to weight: the most extreme Holocaust "revisionists"—Faurisson, Rassinier, Butz[3]—do not deny that *if* the Holocaust had occurred, it would have been an enormity warranting moral reflection, judg-ment, and whatever else followed from these, presumably includ-ing condemnation and punishment; they deny only that it *did* occur. Still more radically and by contrast, Heidegger does not deny that the Nazi genocide against the Jews did occur—only that having occurred, it does not warrant thinking (even *about*). Nor does it lead to further conclusions bearing on moral judgment or historical responsibility (including his own).

Let me first summarize the evidence for claiming that for Heidegger there was no "Jewish Question"—nothing to be thought or said in retrospect about the consummation of the Jewish Question in the Holocaust, nothing that would affect him or his work as he and it stood together in the aftermath of the act of genocide; that would in fact have made the Jewish Question not obsolete but impossible even in its own time. Insofar as my thesis asserts Heidegger's deliberate or thoughtful refusal to think (about) the Holocaust, the primary evidence for this ought to appear in his "thoughtful" work; that is, in the part of his writings ordinarily classified as philosophical rather than popular or public or personal.[4]

To be sure, we face here the problem of ambiguity that confronts any interpretation of silence—in deciding whether the silence (once *that* is demonstrated) had been calculated and deliberate (it might, after all, reflect only indifference or ignorance) and, if it was, what that calculation was. For silence is no less multivalent, no less open to dispute, than words explicitly stated: the silence of horror registering the unspeakable as it mimics the silence of consent; the silence of conspiracy or of pleasure that may be as wordless as the silence of suffering. In still another guise (this has special relevance to Heidegger and the "Jewish Question"), silence may represent a decision not to say what else one would be obliged to say if one spoke at all—contrasted then with the silence of indifference or silence that attests only that the speaker who might have been heard knows too little to say anything about a particular subject; that reflection has, quite simply, been absent. And there can, of course, be other "personal" reasons bearing less on the particular occasion of silence than on the condition of the respondent: psychological causality does not necessarily replicate connections in the external world.

None of these reasons can be excluded as possible explanations of Heidegger's silence on the Holocaust; he himself adds to these the simpler, practical alternative that for him to have spoken on the

Holocaust after the end of the war (the end of the Third Reich) in 1945 would have meant becoming embroiled in discussions and disputes that would have impeded his work—his thinking. Well, perhaps. But that he himself invokes a reason does not mean it is *the* reason or even *a* reason, and indeed I shall be claiming that in his own terms it is the earlier, more substantive consideration—again, his refusal to think the Jewish Question—that explains the absence of any post-Holocaust word from him.

I have already suggested that the problem of interpreting Heidegger's silence does not turn exclusively on the fact or content of what he did not say, since on a few occasions he did mention or refer to the Holocaust. But these citations, in the immediate context of what else he said or did not say, as well as the more extended historical context in which the statements occurred, also reinforce the louder impression of silence. Thus Heidegger's silence becomes more notable because of what he says on the few occasions when he breaks it. Admittedly, the passages we turn to here are as slight as they are well known (they are well known in part *because* they are slight). In some of what they say it is not even certain that they refer to the Nazi genocide against the Jews at all—and we have then to attach a caveat: the statements are as close as Heidegger ever comes to referring to the Holocaust in his formal post-Holocaust writings or teaching. And indeed the record discloses only two such statements, from the second and third of the so-called Bremen lectures (1949):

> Agriculture is now a mechanized food industry, in essence the same as the manufacture of corpses in the gas chambers and extermination camps, the same as the blockade and starvation of the countryside, the same as the production of the hydrogen bombs.[5]

And then:

> Hundreds of thousands die en masse. Do they die? They perish. They are cut down. They become items of material available for the manufacture of corpses. Do they die? Hardly noticed, they are liq-

uidated in extermination camps. And even apart from that, in China millions now perish of hunger.

The lecture in which the first of these statements appeared was later revised and published as "Die Frage nach der Technik" ("The Question concerning Technology"). In that version the statement quoted is radically emended, although it has more recently been published in full;[6] the lecture in which the second statement appears ("Die Gefahr," "The Danger") has now also been published in the volume containing the four Bremen lectures.[7] Both statements, however, are his words—words, moreover, which if he did not later repeat them, he also never retracted, which indeed he never referred to again.

Especially the first of the two statements has drawn comment for the likeness it claims between the mechanization of agriculture and the "manufacturing" of corpses. Admittedly the assertion of this likeness is part of the criticism Heidegger directed *against* one likely outcome (and in his view abuse) of technology. But even this general purpose does not relieve Heidegger of the onus he assumes with his statement: the flagrant disproportion between the two forms of practice for which he claims an essential likeness. It is Heidegger himself who finds in the consequences of an abusive technology no essential difference between the mechanized food industry and "the gas chambers and extermination camp." The likeness is what *he* is claiming, is formed by his perception—even if the likeness then also becomes itself the object of animadversion.

Now, of course analogies are always possible and to that extent unimpeachable; they can be drawn between *any* two objects or practices. It is not this truism, however, that is problematic for the present discussion, but the fact that analogies are themselves also open to evaluation. They are, after all, intended to make—to come to—a point, to establish continuity between two apparently dissimilar objects or events. The likeness asserted is thus meant to be a significant feature in each of the two; the common feature, moreover, is also represented as sufficiently important to warrant consideration in its own right. And on both these points Heidegger's comparison invites challenge—first for the way it ignores the difference between the mechanization of farm labor (presumably for raising food) and the mechanization of killing (in point of fact, for genocide), and then for the abstract concept of technology that he both applies to and finds represented in his analogy. Although less often noted, the analogy Heidegger draws to the "blockade and starvation of the countryside" (the reference is not clear but undoubtedly recalls either the extreme measures the Russian government initiated against parts of its own populace or the "starvation" of the German countryside by Allied, principally Russian, forces) foreshadows the "revisionist" argument that was yet to come: that in the "Final Solution" the Nazis were reacting to fears or at least models defined elsewhere and earlier.[8]

A related objection applies to the second statement, which is, if anything, loftier than the first in its reach for abstraction. The focus here is on what Heidegger distinguishes as two varieties of dying—the one an individual and (supposedly) authentic process, with dying a willful *act*, the other ("perishing") proceeding en masse, mechanically, as something "manufactured." The latter qualities Heidegger ascribes to death in the "extermination camps," implying that in those circumstances death has less authenticity, is somehow less genuine than under the other conditions he mentions. The distinction between the two is meant to be invidious; what is problematic here is thus the abstraction and generalization by which Heidegger hedges the concepts of death and technology, in effect excluding for either of these the likelihood, perhaps even the possibility, of an interior view—the view of a subject. The stance he himself adopts as writer is entirely external, in effect claiming a view articulated so detachedly as to suggest that it is not a view at all.

Even putting aside certain literal-minded questions bearing on the two statements (Why, for example, does Heidegger speak of "hundreds of thousands" dead in the extermination camps and "millions" in the famine of China? Is this a new estimate of the number of victims in the extermination camps? And which Chinese famine is he referring to? Specifically the one following the Communist takeover, or some other? Or is the allusion only a figure of speech? etc., etc.). We return, in any event, to the issue of the substance of the statements: what they leave out, and what is left out around them, as well as what they themselves assert. Let us assume that the two statements do refer to the genocide against the Jews (perhaps to other exterminations as well, with that transferability a part of what is being asserted): Heidegger's audience is given to understand that all the many victims of mass death—whether caused by hunger or natural catastrophe *or* by gas chambers and other varieties of human agency—are alike, that "in essence" they are identical. But what does it mean to make such a claim without first addressing the questions of how those victims came to be victims, who they were, and who *made* them victims? To judge them all "in essence" alike presupposes answers to these questions, certainly presupposes that the questions have been articulated, and more than this, acknowledges that the questions matter. But a reader of the two passages who was unaware that Heidegger had written them after living through—in—the twelve years of Nazi rule might reasonably infer that their author had inhabited a distant land in another age, that he possessed at most second- or third-hand knowledge of the events he refers to, and that because of *this* he would care only academically about their histories (including the question of responsibility, of whose extermination camps they were). For all we know—and revisionist historians would later make just this claim[9]—there would be nothing to distinguish the Nazi death camps from Stalin's Gulag, with the latter serving as a provocation or model and then also justification for the former. Such inference, moreover, yields not merely an objection ad hominem: it is not *his* (Heidegger's) abstraction that is culpable, but the abstraction itself, for which, as it happens, he is responsible.

These references are as close as Heidegger comes to the "Jewish Question" in his formal writings from 1945 on. And few additional references join this brief list even if one moves past the "Jewish Question" to the topic of the Nazi regime as a whole, a regime whose crimes of murder, after all, included millions of non-Jewish victims, including tens of thousands of non-Jewish Germans. There is, of course, the widely cited passage in the *Introduction to Metaphysics* (first presented as lectures in 1935, first published in 1953) in which Heidegger affirms "the inner truth and greatness of this movement" (National Socialism). The dispute over the parenthetical comment that follows this brief endorsement in the 1953 text, specifying what the "inner truth and greatness" *was*—"namely, the encounter between planetary technology and modern man"—and raising the questions of whether the specification was indeed present in Heidegger's original version, as he himself claimed,[10] hardly seems to matter (except as it reflects on the trustworthiness of his other self-descriptions). Indeed, it could be argued that if the parenthetical phrase did appear in the original version, it would have intensified the abstraction that the first phrase represents as left to stand by itself. Certainly the two, joined together, articulate the memory of National Socialism that Heidegger would transmit to the post-Holocaust future. The feature of Nazism he approvingly recalls—Nazism's potentially ideal solution to the "technology question"—is evidently sufficient not only to outweigh but to justify ignoring the Nazis' use of technology, as well as the other practices that appeared in the course of their extravagant history. Certainly he is willing to speak of the former as if it had nothing to do with the latter; the other consequences are, in Heidegger's view, reduced to accidents or mistakes, the merely "external." Thus National Socialism is to be remembered for its potential or ideal "greatness" on the overriding issue of technology—and then also, regretfully, for its failure to realize that potential, to make external the "inner" truth it had promised and of which it evidently had been capable. Once again, then, silence about the "Jewish Question."

Nor do we come any closer to that "Question" when Heidegger reflects on the world war it was part of, even when in that reflection he considers the fate of Germany itself:

> What did the Second World War really decide? (We shall not mention here its fearful consequences for my country, cut in two.) This world war has decided nothing—if we here use "decision" in so high and wide a sense that it concerns solely man's essential fate on this earth.[11]

Inessentially, in other words, we may summon for postwar discussion the division between West and East Germany; essentially, even this does not count—and a fortiori nothing else would, since it must be of still lesser importance.

The explicit and philosophical references to the "Jewish Question" are, then, few; they break the silence only to call attention to it. But there also remain the putatively nonphilosophical writings or statements, those that are more informal (whether conceived with an eye to publication, like the *Spiegel* interview, or not, as in the notable letter that Heidegger wrote in response to Herbert Marcuse). These are, after all, statements in which Heidegger was either provided with or himself contrived an opportunity to address the "Jewish Question" and once again declined to, or came so close to declining as (once again) to underscore the impression of silence. I add this last qualifying clause specifically in the light of his response to Herbert Marcuse, who in the opening letter of his brief postwar correspondence with Heidegger (28 August 1947) challenged the latter's reticence about Nazism in general and about his view of the "Jewish Question" in particular. ("You are still identified with the Nazi regime [that . . . killed millions of Jews—merely because they were Jews]. Many of us have long awaited a statement from you . . . that would clearly and finally free you from such identification.")[12] To this formulation of the "Jewish Question" Heidegger then responds (20 January 1948):

> To the serious legitimate charges that you express "about a regime that murdered millions of Jews . . ." I can merely add that if instead of "Jews" you had written "East Germans," then the same holds true for one of the allies, with the difference that everything that has occurred since 1945 has become public knowledge, while the bloody terror of the Nazis in point of fact had been kept a secret from the German people.

Heidegger's reference here to the "bloody terror of the Nazis" is, I believe, the strongest condemnation of the Nazi regime to appear anywhere in his writings, public or private. This, together with his acknowledgment of the "legitimate charges" that Marcuse made in respect to the millions of Jews murdered, underlies my qualified reference to the "virtual" silence Heidegger maintained even in the face of Marcuse's challenge. It might thus be objected that Heidegger's words here deserve more credit, that they *do* break the silence. And indeed, had these words appeared by themselves, without the severe qualification he immediately attaches to them (a version at best of the tu quoque argument), that objection could hardly be disputed. But the context in which Heidegger sets his comment makes an unavoidable difference, as Marcuse himself notes in his response: to equate what the Nazis did to the Jews with the fate of the ethnic Germans in Poland after the war's end (presumably on the responsibility of the Russians) raises the question of how "a conversation between men is even possible." Should we conclude that Heidegger was by his comparison proposing to add an "East German Question" to the "Jewish Question"? But then we might still ask what the post-Holocaust "Jewish Question" amounts to if Heidegger is able to judge it in the same terms that hold for the expulsion of Germans from the East. (What is at issue is not justifying the latter, but *equating* it with genocide.) One way to make something disappear is to place it, like a grain of sand in the desert, in a mass of supposed likeness—and this is indeed one way Heidegger makes the "Jewish Question" invisible for himself and, by design, for others as well. Whatever else the Holocaust did or did not do, it was not for Heidegger a sufficient reason for distinguishing the Jewish Question even in retrospect.

Two additional documents contribute significantly to the assessment of Heidegger's post-Holocaust stance. Unlike his letter to Marcuse, Heidegger approved these with the awareness that they would eventually be published. This fact, together with the manner of their address, locates them on the boundary between Heidegger's personal or informal discourse and his more professional writings. The first of them—a memorandum written in 1945 and given by Heidegger to his son Hermann for use as he saw fit—was not published until 1983; the second—the *Spiegel* interview—was recorded in 1966 and published in the *Spiegel*, at Heidegger's stipulation, only after his death, in 1976.[13] The two statements are autobiographical in character; they present Heidegger's own view of his Nazi associations, partly responding to specific charges that had been made about those associations, partly as a broader reflection on the period of his life which formally began with his election to the rectorship of the University of Freiburg in April 1933 and which lasted as long as his membership in the Nazi Party; that is, until the end of the war; that is, until the dissolution of the Third Reich marked the involuntary conclusion of that membership. (There is no record—and Heidegger himself did not claim—that he ever resigned.)

Here again our interest in this memorandum and this interview (which also speak of other matters) is with the place in them of the "Jewish Question." Both are "post-Holocaust," formulated after the Jewish Question had been met by the "Final Solution." And also in these two texts that are intended to reflect on, even to judge the past, Heidegger answers the "Jewish Question" with silence. This does not mean he does not allude to Jews or (more rarely) utter the word itself: he does speak the word—six times in the more than forty pages of these documents, specifically intended as the documents are to represent, to *epitomize* his relation to Nazism. In four of those references he cites by its informal title the *Judenplakat* or "Jewish Notice" (meant to be publicly displayed at the university, apparently with twelve theses directed against Jews under the general heading "Against the Un-German Spirit");[14] on the other two occasions he refers, also as a means of identification, to single events or persons, not to the "Jewish Question" as a question. Thus, in the *Spiegel* interview he mentions the "so-called Jewish Notice" that his predecessor as rector had refused to post—to which refusal, he emphasizes, he added his own (although he did not, as he leaves unmentioned, refuse to enforce what it proclaimed: he seems in effect to have been more concerned with the issue of what was posted on university walls than with the particular initiatives that the posters urge).[15] Elsewhere in the same conversation he responds to his *interviewers'* references to Jews. So he denies the charge of having been responsible for the removal of books by Jewish authors from the philosophy library; in response to a question by his interviewers about his treatment of Jewish students, he refers to one student (Helene Weiss) who, when she later received her doctorate at the University of Basel ("this was no longer possible at Freiburg"), included an acknowledgment of thanks to Heidegger in her dissertation; he avoids a direct answer to the question of how the breach between him and Karl Jaspers developed, although denying that it was because of Jaspers's Jewish wife; he offers an explanation on the grounds of philosophical disagreement for breaking off his relationship with his onetime teacher Husserl and a confession of "human failing" in having ignored him and his household at the time of Husserl's last illness and death (1938)—for which, he says, he subsequently apologized to Husserl's wife.[16]

Heidegger makes other, more general references to National Socialism in these two documents, but the allusions cited are the only ones to the terms "Jew" and "Jewish." And in neither the more general nor the specific references as these together represent Heidegger's last will and testament concerning the "Jewish Question"—his *intended* last words (or silence) on that subject—is there evident any judgment or indeed reflection on the historical consequences of National Socialism for the "Jewish Question." Nor is there any judgment that bears on his own history in relation to those policies. Admittedly his interlocutors in the *Spiegel* interview do not force these issues, although they ask at some length about Heidegger's views on other, more general topics including the "condition of the world." Even after they remind Heidegger of his assertion in 1933 that "the Führer and he alone *is* the present and future German reality and its law,"[17] they do not press him to elaborate on his explanation that these words appeared in a "local Freiburg student paper," that as rector he knew he would have to make certain "compromises," that he "would not write those words today [1966!]," and that already in 1934 he "did not say them."

In "The Rectorat 1933/34: Facts and Thoughts," the document he entrusted to his son in 1945, Heidegger also alludes to his resistance to posting the "Jewish Notice" and mentions the spontaneous silence with which an audience of which he was part reacted to a lecture on race by a Nazi official during the period cited.[18] He also refers to his Rectoral Address and to other more professional writings from the same period and the period soon after his resignation, emphasizing what he alleges was the hostile reaction to them by Nazi orthodoxy. (That alleged reaction bears considerable weight in these and others of his apologetics; his emphasis on it is evidently meant to demonstrate the *difference* between him and other adherents of the party—a difference that Nazi officialdom itself [also allegedly] regarded with suspicion.) But once again, either during the period 1933–34 or in the subsequent outcome of that "Question," nothing more is said about the "Jewish Question" than what has been indicated.

One last document with quasi-official standing should be mentioned here—a letter, dated 4 November 1945, in which Heidegger requested that the rector of the University of Freiburg act to reinstate him on the faculty. (This followed an initial decision in the "denazification" process barring him from the university.) Heidegger's statement in this document has a narrower purpose than the other two thus far cited in the second category of "public writings"; perhaps this makes the absence from it of any general reference to the "Jewish Question" less egregious. Indirectly, however, his apologia is more specific and substantive than in the other statements, as he calls attention to what he claims as his early (and, he would have it, continuing) dissent from the orthodox version of Nazi biological racism. Glossing a passage in the Rectoral Address (27 May 1933) in which he asserted that "The greatness of a Volk is guaranteed by its spiritual world values," he now contends (in 1945) that "for those who know and think, these sentences express my opposition to [Alfred] Rosenberg's conception, according to which, conversely, spirit and the world of spirit are merely an 'expression' . . . of racial facts and of the physical constitution of man." In a later passage of this same letter, he reiterates his (then) opposition to "the dogmatism and primitivism of Rosenberg's biologism."[19]

As I argue more fully in chapter 4, contrary to what has often been held (also, evidently, by Heidegger), such statements do not in themselves controvert the charges either of racism or, more specifically, of antisemitism—since even for Nazi antisemitism and still more obviously for the varieties of antisemitism preceding it, the biological ground was but one among a number of elements (pre-Mendelian antisemitism was antisemitism nonetheless). Moreover (this too will be elaborated), Heidegger's endorsement in the same context where these statements appear of the principle of the Volk as based on *spiritual* grounds reflects a basic and consistent line in his thinking, one that had been responsible, as I shall claim, for his silence on the Jewish Question also at a time when the Question itself was quite real. And furthermore, even as he purports to have rejected specific elements of Nazi orthodoxy, his emphasis is on the (alleged) reaction of the Nazi hierarchy *to his views*—not on the other actions of the Nazi regime that were going on all around him that may or may not have conflicted with those views; and not on the specific consequences directly associated with the Nazi concept of the Volk for which the biological ground was but one, and to *other* grounds of which Heidegger had been and arguably remained committed.

In addition to the available documents cited that fall into this second category of evidence (Heidegger's "public" or personal— in contrast to his professional—writings), there almost certainly are others in the second category and perhaps also in the first that may yet become known among the still (and as of now, indefinitely) closed Heidegger papers in the German Literary Archives at Marbach. (The stipulation guarding the Heidegger papers is that access is permitted only to those manuscripts that have already been published; the executors who determine what will be published thus have control first and last.) But although the possibility cannot be ruled out, there is no reason to believe that the archives contain anything that would amount to a retraction or significant qualification of the statements by Heidegger that have been mentioned or even a fuller analysis of his possible objections to introducing such changes.[20] In the absence of this evidence, at any rate, the conjunction of "personal" and "philosophical" statements that have been cited gives weight to the claim that for Heidegger the "Jewish Question" (that is, the Jewish Question seen through the lens of the Holocaust) had been ruled out deliberately (that is, thoughtfully) and for his own purposes effectively.

An objection might be raised against this assembly of evidence concerning "Heidegger and the 'Jewish Question'" that draws on two points already mentioned. The first of these is Heidegger's own contention that much of his philosophical writing was oppositional, clearly (if only by implication) directed against Nazi doctrine. This is again his own reading of his Rectoral Address in respect to Rosenberg's biological racism; a similar claim appears in the same 1945 letter in which he asks for reinstatement at Freiburg, when he recalls his writing and lecturing on Nietzsche as also a gesture of dissent:

> It is unjust to assimilate Nietzsche to National Socialism, an assimilation which—apart from what is essential—ignores his hostility to anti-Semitism and his positive attitude with respect to Russia. But on a higher plane, the debate with Nietzsche's metaphysics is a debate with nihilism as it manifests itself with increased clarity under the political form of fascism.[21]

Again, the detail of this passage raises questions about what constitutes a defense. Heidegger never, early *or* late, disguised his antagonism to communism and Russia; thus his exposition of Nietzsche, who as it happens—it has very little bearing on Heidegger's analysis—refers to Russia positively, represented no change in Heidegger's opinion on *that* count. Why then should a reader believe that Heidegger, by his emphasis on Nietzsche's general philosophical significance, demonstrates approval of Nietzsche's attacks on antisemitism?

But more important: Even if one accepts Heidegger's construal of his own writings as tacitly oppositional, the evidence on which he bases this claim dates from the period of Nazi rule. If he felt obliged at *that* time to write obliquely, between the lines—in effect joining the philosophical tradition that Leo Strauss characterizes in *Persecution and the Art of Writing*[22]—he faced no similar danger after the war's end when he called his readers' attention to that earlier coded opposition. Why, if he had indeed previously objected, but in so veiled a way as to leave himself open to misinterpretation, would he not, in arguing for his own retrospective view of himself, speak out explicitly in the new present, during the thirty years when he faced no similar threat of punishment or censure? Certainly he could have said then with impunity what perhaps justifiably or excusably he had hesitated to say before. Was the reason for the later silence identical to or different from the reason for the earlier one? (And this, of course, bypasses the question of how much weight to give Heidegger's reading of his own texts in the first place; his glosses of himself seem no less contestable at times—in fact and method—than certain of his readings of *other* writers.)

The second point joining this first one is the difficult question (again) of how silence is to be interpreted. For even if the thesis asserted here were accepted for the sake of argument—that after allowing for whatever Heidegger says about the "Jewish Question" we find the whole still amounting to a denial—the silence in itself remains ambiguous, expressing a variety of possible motives or implications. As mentioned before, one interpretation of this ambiguity has argued that precisely Heidegger's silence on the issue at hand constitutes an expressive and significant response *just as* silence—since in respect to certain profound questions, it might be held (and Heidegger himself did) that silence is itself all that can be "said" about them, the meaning of the silence itself then also attesting to the centrality of the questions.[23] Here silence is not something that can be replaced by words (that is, a silence of omission), but a space in which silence *is* the answer.

How much do we know, in other words, even if we agree that for Heidegger there was no "Jewish Question"? I have acknowledged that this silence does not by itself imply that he chose to exclude the "Question": the latter might not have occurred to him—or he might have avoided it not because of what *it* entailed, but because in addressing it, he would have had also to speak about other matters that he preferred to avoid. And there again, would he not, like any other author, have been within his rights?

I suggested earlier that we may be able to advance on this issue by considering the occasions, public or private, when intimations of the "Jewish Question" are in fact expressed by Heidegger; a number of these occasions have been cited—with these too (so I claim) affirming the predominant silence, underscoring it as meditated, deliberate. An additional (third) category of evidence for the latter thesis appears in what Heidegger was at the same time thinking and writing about *other* questions (or even "questions"). He was not, after all, silent through and through; he spoke and wrote widely and at length, and the absence of an issue or a question can often best be understood by considering what else was present. Such other discussion can disclose a basis for the exclusion of whatever was excluded; or it might lead us to reassess the supposed "fact" of that exclusion. In any event, the silence by itself is inconclusive.

Well, perhaps. And indeed, in following the progression from Heidegger's first silence on the Jewish Question to his later silence on the "Jewish Question," I shall refer more directly to what Heidegger *was* saying while at the same time he maintained the earlier silence. It is certainly arguable, in fact, that the more crucial test of Heidegger's views will be there, in his pre-Holocaust writing, without the pressure that his own knowledge of subsequent history (both Nazi history and his own) would later exert on him and—so far as it is possible—without being read by way of our own post-Holocaust consciousness. Even without adding such earlier and steadier references to the balance, however, one can grant all the possibilities mentioned and still insist that his silence on the "Jewish Question" must weigh heavily, no matter what else he had said or was yet to say about other questions or issues. Heavily, because it was itself deliberate, thoughtful, *chosen*. Derrida writes about Heidegger's silence that "It leaves us the commandment to think what he did not think."[24] And does it not make a difference in what we are commanded to think that it was by thinking, not its absence, that Heidegger chose silence?

When Heidegger writes in his letter to Marcuse that "a confession after 1945 was impossible for me, because the Nazi partisans announced their change of allegiance in the most loathsome way; and I, however, had nothing in common with them," we have a further glimpse of what he saw as his own motives for silence (this glimpse implies that a "confession" would have been warranted, but that other considerations in the end overrode that justification).

If he had condemned the genocide of the Jews—by itself or joined to other Nazi crimes—he fears that he would have been mistaken for those other "partisans" of Nazism who lacked his own thoughtful and sophisticated commitment. Those others could more easily shed their earlier allegiance because that allegiance had itself been easier, more superficial, based perhaps only on psychological or practical grounds. In his own view, then, Heidegger's objection to breaking his silence reflects the wish to have his own history accurately distinguished (in addition, as we earlier saw, to avoiding the disruption of his work). In maintaining the silence, however, which here at least he himself acknowledges, he is obviously willing to risk the misunderstandings *it* may produce. For is it not evident that to remain silent at certain times also poses dangers? That such dangers can be as large as those chanced in breaking the silence?

But also in respect to the latter questions, distinct and ominous as they are, Heidegger is silent—apparently willing to face the dangers of silence whatever the consequences. And since Heidegger also makes *this* choice in silence, we are left to wonder in retrospect whether he recognized the risk of his now twofold silence as a risk at all. It is possible—likely, I conclude—that the dangers he chanced here seemed to him entirely on the other side. That is, only if he broke the silence, only if he were to speak about the subject he was denying—and before that, as he would himself insist, only if he were to think it.

CHAPTER THREE

Heidegger When the
Jewish Question Still Was

Recently I got a second invitation to teach at the University of Berlin. On that occasion I left Freiburg and withdrew to the cabin. I listened to what the mountains and the forest and the farmlands were saying, and I went to see an old friend of mine, a 75-year-old farmer. He had read about the call to Berlin in the newspaper. What would he say? Slowly he fixed the sure gaze of his clear eyes on mine, and keeping his mouth tightly shut, he thoughtfully put his faithful hand on my shoulder. Ever so slightly he shook his head. That meant: absolutely no.

Martin Heidegger, "Why We Remain in the Provinces"
(7 March 1934)

O NE WAY OF UNDERSTANDING the present—silent or not—is to look at the past, and that is at once the method and the contention in this second part of my discussion. Thus, to understand why for Heidegger there was no "Jewish Question," we look back to a time when the Jewish Question had an indisputable presence, when it was addressed repeatedly and in so many words by both Jews and non-Jews, antisemites and philosemites, outside Germany as much as inside. This is not the place to follow the history of that Question to its origins, to see the way that modernity would in its own time make manifest what had been latent—concrete, but still latent—for centuries before. Of course peoples and religions had lived side by side, over or under each other, long before the Enlightenment and its revolutionary advocates confounded them with talk about "the rights of man" and then, in mingled deference to the state, about "civil rights." But this amalgam of rights posed issues for the traditional boundaries of group identity that made it virtually impossible for those boundaries themselves not to be disputed, from inside and outside—mainly through the practical question of who should be accorded rights, of what kind, and to what extent.

It was not the Jews alone, of course, who were implicated in this question; most European countries included other minorities as well, some of them living as close to the national margins as the Jews did. But because by the eighteenth century versions of the ghetto or (a bit later) the "pale" had replaced the outright ban in most of Europe and the New World, the Jews had come to live in many places and many kinds of places, adapting themselves to the fit of regulations as different as those of the French monarchy and of czarist Russia, but in almost all their habitats representing in their persons a special case. Thus the Jewish Question emerged in force partly as a matter of repetition, asserted in each of the European countries as they found themselves compelled to rethink the notion of citizenship in terms other than those that preceded it, with fealty or subordination to authority as their basis and only then going on to grant (or deny) any rights—that is, "rights."

The details of this process would be proportionately complex—tied both to national histories (whose writing was itself still in process) and to local histories caught up in eddies of the same current.[1] But it would not have been necessary for a twentieth-century German philosopher to move far outside his own professional interests to meet the Jewish Question, since the latter was not only or even primarily directed at historians. Admittedly, the turns and twists of emancipation—impelling the complex decisions about who was to have which rights and where and when—were and would remain matters of historical finding and fact. But a still larger issue in the Jewish Question was, for better or worse, a matter of principle: What *are* civil rights, and then who should have them (or not have them, or partly have them)? These questions imposed themselves not only on legislators but, evoking the national culture as a whole, on anyone—poets, the clergy, the new industrialists—for whom a corporate unity might provide a means as well as an incentive. Certainly the Enlightenment and post-Enlightenment history of German philosophers would be at home with the idiom—and thus it was no accident that for figures such as Lessing, Herder, and Fichte (albeit in different ways), the Jewish Question occupied a significant place in the "anthropological" thinking close to the center of their concerns.[2] If the status of the nation or the "people"—and so also the Jewish Question—was less prominent in Kant and Hegel, this was more a matter of proportion, reflecting the larger dimensions of their thinking, than of indifference, since they too found occasions for referring to them, both the general and the particular.

In other words, had Heidegger lived only within the confines of the history of philosophy, and in that history within the part of it closest to his own history, the Jewish Question—the status of nations in general and, in specific relation to that, the status of this one "repetitive" nation—would have been not only real but visible, in effect unavoidable. Furthermore, it is obvious that neither the Question nor Heidegger himself lived only within the boundaries of philosophy's domain. For elsewhere as well, and as much there or more—in the law courts and legislatures, in commerce, in the academy as in other public institutions—the Jewish Question was a continuing presence, partly in expressions of self-assertion or ressentiment (both of these contributed), but still more basically as the shifting lines of group identity even from within forced attention to it. The Question itself then remained poised, mirroring the edge of other local and national political changes; it was, not alone but also, connected to them.

Something like this state of affairs would be required to explain how the "Jewish Question" as an expression would appear in its multinational and multilingual forms. More important, its presence—in Poland and England, in Prussia and the Netherlands, in nascent Italy and imperial Austro-Hungary—was constant and unmistakable. When systemic (and nationalist) antisemitism began to gain force in the second half of the nineteenth century, as contact between ethnic groups increased and as the biological and linguistic "sciences" fed the emerging concepts of race, the "Jewish Question" became increasingly charged—and Austria and Germany, together with France, were central staging areas for this development. The general issues of citizenship, of individual and group rights, could not be kept out of public view, if only because the issues themselves *were* public. One need not claim that the Jewish Question was central or crucial in the general consciousness to recognize that it was recurrent and evident, a peculiarly constant element among social issues of the day, for the Jewish communities of Europe and the Americas, in effect for all the "host" countries in which Jews lived. And this held as well for the largely Catholic district of Baden where Heidegger was born and educated as for other districts of Germany.

I have claimed, however, that also in the period before and during the Holocaust, there was no Jewish Question for Heidegger in his philosophical work, and that this absence, with the issue itself historically and contemporaneously present—*real*—requires explanation. I mean to argue further that to understand this earlier stage is to understand why, consistently, there would be no "Jewish Question" for Heidegger after the Holocaust. This causal claim may seem overstated: except on the assumptions of historical determinism with their a priori wistfulness, the sequences of individual histories, after all, are no more "necessary" than those of corporate history on a larger and more impersonal scale. Yet even after leaving room for discontinuities in historical explanation, the search persists in historiography for patterns of association and causality—and Heidegger's own version of his history will hardly be immune to that same scrutiny.

The issue of what is to count as evidence is more complex in this stage of the argument than in the first one. For here (I refer to anything in Heidegger's voice before 1945 that bears on the Jewish Question) the two categories of evidence so far considered—the first composed of his "philosophical" statements, the second, of his public or personal statements—are more extensive in both space

and time. (Again, it is part of my thesis that the distinction between these is for Heidegger a distinction without a difference, but
this remains to be shown.) And two additional, albeit quite different, categories become pertinent as well: a third that includes
whatever *else* Heidegger was saying ("philosophical" or not) that
might then or later preclude reference to the Jewish Question or
otherwise explain its absence; and a fourth that becomes more important before 1945, minus the added weight of Holocaust history,
than subsequently—the occasional secondhand reports of what
Heidegger did or said during that time (again, as pertinent to either of the first two categories). These last reports, mainly of conversations with Heidegger recalled by another party to those
conversations, but also of impressions conveyed to them by others,
have the status of hearsay; but since the credibility of the witnesses
can be judged independently, there is no reason to disregard this
testimony out of hand.

Thus, once again, back to the texts themselves—now in reference to Heidegger and the Jewish Question (unframed by quotation marks), considering the relation of Jews to the nations,
whether in general or a particular one. And here again the evidence in the first category of Heidegger's philosophical writings is
easily summarized, more so even than his few words on the "Jewish Question." There is, quite simply, nothing at all in the way of
direct reference to the Jews—not in the major works of *Being and
Time* or *The Basic Problems of Phenomenology* or *Contributions to Philosophy*; and not in the shorter essays like "On the Essence of
Truth" or the *Introduction to Metaphysics*, some of which, although
written or spoken during this time, were published only later, after
the war's end.[3]

Well, what then? That question also repeats itself, now with a
sharper edge, since one might assert here more forcefully than in
respect to the later writings that from such silence nothing follows.
Indeed, that given their subjects—Being, Time, Truth—it would be
unwarranted to expect, let alone require, reference in them to the
status of the Jews in Germany or anyplace else. Heidegger was not,
after all, writing cultural criticism or sociology, not even political
or social theory: Why then, unless the issue had been somehow

forced on him, as it evidently was not, *would* he consider the Jewish Question?

This prima facie objection loses at least some of its strength, however, when measured by what Heidegger *was* speaking and writing about during this time in the (second) category of his "public" or "personal" writings. For here we again find a break in the silence of his more strictly philosophical writings. And although explicit references are infrequent in these sources too, enough of them occur to be symptomatic—especially as we juxtapose them to the subjects that he *was* addressing in his philosophical work and to the views he expressed on them. Once again the few explicit references in his public or personal writings have been widely cited; it is a matter, then, of reassembling them. (Although I mention these here, I discuss several at greater length in the next chapter, in relation to the matter of Heidegger's antisemitism.)

Thus two Heidegger letters exist that refer to the philosopher Eduard Baumgarten, once a favored student of Heidegger's but about whose qualifications Heidegger later changed his mind. In the first letter (2 October 1929), when he still was confident of Baumgarten's promise, Heidegger asks that Baumgarten be given a stipend at Freiburg—because, Heidegger writes, a choice must be made between those who would contribute to the "forces and educators of our German intellectual life" and those who would further its "Jewification" (*Verjudung*). In the second letter, written after his opinion of Baumgarten changed (dated 16 December 1933, during his rectorship), Heidegger, attempting to scuttle Baumgarten's proposed appointment at Göttingen, charges that Baumgarten had been associated in the past with "liberal-democratic intellectuals" and with "the Jew [Eduard] Fränkel." The terms "Jewification" and "Jew" are obviously meant to be sufficient for both identification and derogation; that Heidegger uses the two references for contradictory purposes in respect to Baumgarten underscores the terms' own common connotation. This impression intensifies with the possibility suggested by Baumgarten himself (see the Luban memoir in the Appendix) that Heidegger *invented* Baumgarten's association with Fränkel, whom Baumgarten in fact did not know, in order to avoid naming and so provoking a confrontation with Husserl, who had indeed befriended Baumgarten.[4] In an official statement that he issued as rector a few days before the second Baumgarten letter (13 December 1933), Heidegger sought signatures and financial contributions for a manifesto of Nazi ideology that was then to be sent to foreign universities under the title "Appeal to All the Educated People of the World." Heidegger repeats there the stipulation that had accompanied the request *he* had received to circulate the Appeal: "It goes without saying that non-Aryans will not appear among the signatories."[5]

Now IT MIGHT BE objected that these references are few and limited; that they fail to conceptualize (and so also to deny) the Jewish Question in any systematic way; that they verge on a conventional or stereotyped antisemitism with no theoretical implications at all. To this extent they would leave Heidegger's silence on the Jewish Question no less ambiguous than his silence on the "Jewish Question," with the significance of each of these open to interpretation not only initially but later as well. Certainly in comparison with other statements from the same period—those found, for example, not only in the popular antisemitic rhetoric of a publication such as *Der Völkische Beobachter*, but in the "professional" writing of other academics (including the philosophers who hewed most closely to the Nazi line like Alfred Bäumler and Ernst Krieck)[6]—Heidegger's statements, although hardly innocuous, appear subdued.

Such contextualization often appears in the service of apologetics, of normalizing a discourse, and that is a possible use to which also of these last comments might be put. But to justify (or challenge) that function, the process itself—locating Heidegger's statements on the Jewish Question in their then current historical setting and against the background of his other writing and thinking—would have to be detailed. Even before attempting this, however, it seems pertinent to note briefly a number of contemporary (*also* pre-1945) impressions of Heidegger vis-à-vis the Jewish Question (the fourth category of evidence mentioned above). Again Heidegger's appearance in these accounts comes filtered through intermediary reporters who are hardly "disinterested" (whatever it could mean to be disinterested on that issue at that time). But for the discussion of Heidegger and the Jewish Question, the impression these observers convey of his denial of the Question is significant—the more so when they cite encounters that took place before it was clear to Heidegger (or to them) what the outcome of Nazi ambitions would be and the extremes they would reach. These accounts too seem in themselves isolated and slight, but what they are representations of is neither.

So, for example, Karl Löwith, whom Heidegger had "habilitated" at Marburg in 1928, writes in a memoir about his 1936 meeting with Heidegger in Rome where the "half-Jewish" Löwith was living precariously in exile:

> Even on this occasion Heidegger had not removed the Party insignia from his jacket. . . . It had apparently not occurred to him that the swastika was out of place when spending a day with me. . . . I . . . explained to him that . . . it was my opinion that a partisanship for National Socialism lay in the essence of his philosophy. Heidegger agreed with me without reservation. . . . He also left no doubt about his belief in Hitler. According to him, Hitler had underestimated only two things: the vitality of the Christian churches and the obstacles to the Anschluss of Austria. . . . Only the excessive organizing at the expense of vital energies seemed questionable to him.[7]

Or again, Karl Jaspers reports on a conversation with Heidegger at the time of an official visit by the latter to the University of Heidelberg in May 1933: "I told him that he was expected to stand up for the university and its great tradition. No answer. I referred to the Jewish Question ('Judenfrage') and the malicious nonsense about the sages of Zion. He replied: 'There really is a dangerous international fraternity of Jews.'"[8]

Again, however credible their sources, these statements have the weakened force of third-party reports. But the evidence they suggest about Heidegger's attitude toward the Jewish Question becomes more explicit in the testimony of what Heidegger *was* writing and saying in this same pre-Holocaust period—what he was asserting apart from the Jewish Question that nonetheless reflected on it. Indeed, it is mainly this evidence that establishes his silence (anticipating his silence on the "Jewish Question") as intentional and deliberate: *thoughtful*. For that silence turns out, I would claim, to be the obverse of what Heidegger was discussing and asserting during this period, blatantly in his public formulations but more systematically (and in the end no less explicitly) also in his philosophical writings. And what he was asserting in the latter, I would argue, is no less fundamental than what determines his silence in the former.

It is striking that in none of Heidegger's public statements during his year-long tenure as rector does he openly refer to Jews or to the Jewish Question; indeed, there is no *explicit* reference to the racial doctrines of the Nazis in any of their standard formulations—no elaboration of the quasi-scientific grounds the Nazis based them on or of the goal of racial purification they were designed to achieve. In the context of the time, this consistent absence in Heidegger's public writing and speaking is extremely unlikely to have been accidental. It has been inferred—and he himself was later to claim—that this absence (in his own terms, refusal) was in itself oppositional: to be silent on central themes of public discourse must count as a demurral. This conclusion would follow, however, only if what Heidegger *was* saying or writing at the time were, if not also oppositional, at least devoid of other support for the Nazi ideology in its implications for the Jewish Question. And this is markedly *not* the case. For at the same time that he was tacitly contesting Nazi racial doctrine on its biological grounds (if we accept his self-interpretation, or even if we credit only the more modest claim that he was not a biological determinist) Heidegger's thinking and writing nonetheless advocated an alternative version of racism that is no less pointed and severe in its implications. In one sense this other version is potentially even more dangerous than the first, because it comes unburdened by the pseudoscientific biological ground that makes the first so vulnerable to criticism. It is about this extrascientific context that Derrida puts to Heidegger the quasi-rhetorical question, "Is a metaphysics of race more or less serious than a naturalism or biologism of race?"[9]

I refer here, then, to Heidegger's repeated emphasis on the status of the "Volk" in general and of the German "Volk" in particular, as he claims for those respective collectives an intrinsic determination or essence (hence also destiny), then going on to an invidious contrast between the German Volk and other "peoples" because of the former's privileged access to Being and Truth. I believe it can be shown that these claims, although not logically *entailed* from grounds provided in the conceptual structure of Heidegger's work, are contextually embedded there; that they are more than just consistent with the basic (and continuing) principles of his work—that they are disposed toward the latter. Certainly the roles assigned to the Volk—and then to the German Volk—are neither incidental nor independent within the framework of his thinking, as has sometimes been inferred from the contention that his references to those roles appear only in his public or political speeches and writing. In point of fact that contention is itself refuted by the evidence: those concepts appear in Heidegger's more strictly philosophical work, at once closely resembling the concepts at work in his more obviously public pronouncements and yet systematically motivated within the philosophical texts themselves, not borrowed or echoed. This seems to me further evidence for the *converse* thesis: that the status assigned the Volk in Heidegger's designedly public or political discourse stems from a deeper metaphysical ground, weighing against the claim that the stereotyping and (supposed) lack of rigor in those public utterances reflect only opportunistic and spontaneous impulses which ought then to be discounted or at least judged apart from his "real" thinking. Thus do the two categories of "philosophical" and of "public" or "personal" evidence converge.

The case to be made, then, begins with certain of the public statements:

> The [German] Volk [thus] recaptures the truth of its will to existence, because truth is the disclosure of that which makes a Volk sure, bright, and strong in its transactions and its knowledge. From such a source, science arises for us; it is linked to the necessity of the autonomous existence of a Volk.[10]

The so-called "spiritual labor" is that not because it involves "higher spiritual things" but because *as labor* it reaches more deeply into the need of the historical existence of a Volk, driven there more immediately—because more knowingly—by the severity of the danger of human existence.[11]

Again, such statements might be judged merely instances of popular rhetoric and so manifestations (in the writer's own view or in his conception of his audience's view) of prejudice or thoughtlessness—to be contrasted with Heidegger's deeper, more genuinely philosophical thinking. But this defense loses credibility when we find in what must be acknowledged to be his *philosophical* writings the same privileging of the German Volk:

Only from the Germans can world historical mediation come—provided that they find and defend what is German.[12]

The peril of world . . . darkening . . . [will] be forestalled [only] if our nation in the center of the Western world is to take on its historical mission.[13]

We are caught in a pincers. Situated in the middle, our Volk experiences the severest pressure. It is the Volk with the most neighbors and hence the most endangered—and with all this, the metaphysical Volk. We are certain of this mission. But the Volk will only be able to realize that destiny if *within itself* it creates a resonance . . . and takes a creative view of its heritage. All this implies that this Volk, as a historical Volk, must move itself and thereby the history of the West beyond the center of their future "happening" and *into the primordial realm of the powers of Being*.[14]

To be sure, at certain points Heidegger emphasizes the role of the "Volk" in its general form—not the *German* Volk; or he speaks of the German Volk without invidious comparison with other peoples. But also in these instances, the same issue of evidence arises—What grounds are there for the claims made? So, for example:

This historical Volk [Germany] has already triumphed and is un-conquerable if it remains the nation of poets and thinkers that it is essentially, as long as it does not fall victim to the dreadful—because always threatening—deviation from, and thus misunder-standing of, its essence.[15]

Reflection on the Volk is an essential stage. . . . An uppermost rung of Being will be attained if a "Völkisch principle," as something determinative, is mastered and brought into play for historical Da-sein.[16]

The "Fatherland" is Being itself, which from the ground up carries and ordains the history of a Volk as one that exists: the historicity of its history.[17]

Certain statements referring to the concept of the Volk point only by implication to the *German* Volk; so, in the Rectoral Address (which stands uneasily on the border between his "political" and the "philosophical" discourses):

And the *spiritual world* of a people [Volk] is not the superstructure of a culture, no more than it is an armory stuffed with useful facts and values; it is the power that most deeply preserves the people's strengths, which are tied to earth and blood; and as such it is the power that most deeply moves and most profoundly shakes its be-ing (*Dasein*). Only a spiritual world gives the people the assurance of greatness.[18]

Perhaps, again, it will be objected that Heidegger's conception of the Volk in such passages is only a reversion to nationalist rhetoric that may then be judged simply as emotive or personal ex-pression, at any rate as distinct from his "metaphysical" thinking. But it is important to keep in mind that the sources in which the passages cited appear are, by any standard that is not circular (that would not rule them out just *because* of what they say), among Hei-degger's philosophical works, not his "political" or public works. Again, to defend the latter distinction by claiming that wherever

Heidegger makes a statement bearing on political or social conditions, we know *by that fact* that the statement stands apart from his deeper or more authentic "philosophical" position must beg the question.

Even if the echoes of a standard nationalistic rhetoric are recognizable in such passages, moreover—for which earlier and no less prominent German sources could be cited, especially in Herder but also in Fichte and Schelling—it seems clear that both for Heidegger and for those other figures, more than "political" nationalism is at issue. Certainly Heidegger means to distinguish his concept of the Volk from the appearances of that concept among the garden varieties of nationalism. So in the "Letter on Humanism" (itself written in 1946–47 but here referring to a 1943 text he had written on Hölderlin), Heidegger elaborates on his own use of the term *Heimat* ("homeland"): "The word is thought here in an essential sense, not patriotically or nationalistically but in terms of the history of Being."[19] Or again, in an earlier statement from a political address, one that is the more telling because of its matter-of-fact tone in reciting categories and numbers evidently assumed to be beyond dispute: "Eighteen million Germans belong to the Volk but, because they are living outside the borders of the Reich, do not yet belong to the Reich."[20] That the "ethnic" Germans (*Volksdeutsch*) he refers to were formally citizens of other nations apparently made no more difference to Heidegger's inclusion of them in the German Volk than did the fact that more than a half million German (and German-speaking) Jews who had been full German citizens were at this time being deprived of their citizenship (to say nothing of their exclusion from the Volk).

There is, I believe, no alternative to concluding from such statements that a concept like "homeland" and, more prominently, the concept of the Volk as inhabiting it are based not on political or legal or biological categories—singly or together—but on metaphysical ones, exceeding the empirical limits of these other categories and themselves attached to, disclosing, Being. Historical and linguistic origins and traditions no doubt pertain to the latter source in Heidegger's thinking, but exactly what he considers to individuate the concepts, defining criteria of inclusion or exclusion and thus of identity, remains obscure and indeed unspoken. That Heidegger frequently invokes the idea of a spirit (*Geist*) or an essence (*Wesen*)—applicable to the idea of a Volk or of the German Volk in particular, as in the passages cited above—is a mark of the metaphysical ground on which those expressions rest. The latter conclusion does not by itself discredit the concepts, but it imposes a requirement, in Heidegger's own terms, for at least "metaphysical" explanation and evidence. And these he neither provides nor attempts to provide. We find a symptomatic expression of this confusing referent in the odd collection of components that Heidegger assembles in a passing definition of the Volk, one of the few places where he attempts to describe its features: "the communal, the racial, the base and subordinate, the national, the enduring."[21] He elsewhere also proposes a substantial role for philosophy itself in the formation of a Volk: "A historical Volk without philosophy is like an eagle without the high expanse of the glowing ether, wherein its soaring attains its highest flight."[22]

Just how systematically problematic the role of the German Volk is for him (and by implication, though to a lesser extent, the role of the Volk as such) becomes dramatically evident in the applications Heidegger finds for it, most revealingly in relation to the German language and the German capacity for philosophy. Thus even as late and openly as the 1966 *Spiegel* interview—by which time there could be no doubt about the provocation that any drawing of an invidious "essential" line between the Germans and other peoples would constitute—Heidegger responds to the interviewer's question whether the Germans have any "specific qualification" for affecting the present condition of the world: "I think of the special inner relation between the German language and the language of the Greeks and of thinking. This, the French continually confirm for me. When they begin to think, they speak German; they assure [me] that they would not succeed in their own language."[23] Or in the earlier *Introduction to Metaphysics*, as he recalls the precedent in classical Greek for the (allegedly) modern preeminence of German: "Along with German, the Greek language is (in regard to its possibilities for thought) at once the most powerful and most spiritual of all languages."[24]

What exactly is it in the nature or history of a people or a language that would produce this enabling capacity—or that, by its absence, would prevent others from achieving it? In Derrida's concise formulation, "Why this incommensurable privilege of one language?"[25] It has been argued that even in a central section of his Rectoral Address, where he quotes a line from Aeschylus, and then builds on his translation, Heidegger was willing to sacrifice linguistic history for the philosophical point offered by the context—and though the issue of translation is separate from the issue of what grounds there could be for privileging one language *essentially* over others, the willfulness in respect to the status of (the) language seems a common element in those several references.[26] Typically, the common source comes grounded in his etymological searches of Greek or German or Old English—with the histories of the words singled out there (e.g., *doxa, bin, thanc*)[27] according privileged status to originary meaning. Why *that* is the case, however—since it is not obvious that first meaning (chronologically) is or ought to be dominant—or why the languages he searches in are privileged over other languages, Heidegger does not discuss or argue. Nor does he take account of the developmental history of the German language—even, as Hegel had noted, in relation to philosophy itself; so the goal that was for Hegel yet to be achieved: "I shall try to teach philosophy to speak German. Once that is accomplished, it will be infinitely more difficult to give shallowness the appearance of profound speech."[28]

That Heidegger himself had access only to certain languages is understandable; but this condition does not, of course, provide an ontological warrant for those or any other languages (or a basis for comparing them with "all [other] languages"). Perhaps at their first historical appearance certain terms are indeed more closely in touch with Thinking or Being than their successors; perhaps certain languages are better adapted than others for certain purposes; perhaps some or all linguistic systems carry implicit metaphysical commitments (so, for example, Whitehead argues for the origins of philosophical dualism in the subject-predicate structure identified in Aristotle's analysis of the proposition).[29] And perhaps, as related to any of these differing linguistic capacities, the speakers of one language—a particular "Volk"—may by that fact have a readier disposition or talent than other speakers for certain practices or achievements. But by even moderate requirements of evidence, these claims are large and disputable, and Heidegger neither acknowledges their challenge nor offers evidence for the specific conclusions he draws. (Some of his own linguistic analyses and translations have been seriously disputed, including his rendering of the concluding quotation from Plato's *Republic* in the Rectoral Address.)[30] The assertion of a special affinity between the Germans and the Greeks was, of course, no innovation of Heidegger's. From their roots in nineteenth-century German aesthetics and linguistics, the widespread claims in Germany for that association had also reached philosophy proper. Indeed, although not necessarily for the same reasons, other Nazi philosophers were no less ready than Heidegger to assume the same affinity—thus making less startling than it otherwise might seen Hans Sluga's statement that for the Nazi philosophers "Plato became the most authoritative political thinker and the *Republic* the most widely read work on political theory."[31]

There is surely *something* in Heidegger's reference to the Volk-concept of the kitsch exemplified in the epigraph at the beginning of this chapter, where Heidegger finds a reason for not leaving Freiburg for Berlin in the eyes—and silence—of a Schwarzwald farmer. And the connotations of *Volk* and *völkisch* do indeed leave room for Heidegger's discovery in them (and in other formulations as well) of the distinctive value of rural and peasant life, of attachment and access to the land. So, for example, his assumption in the influential essay "The Origin of the Work of Art" that the "peasant woman's shoes" in a Van Gogh painting had been shaped by their wearer in her toil—shoes that turn out, as Meyer Schapiro would then show, to have almost certainly been Van Gogh's own. Or again: "Man tries in vain to bring the globe to order through planning, when he is not in tune with the consoling voice of the country lane"[32]—and as concisely as it *could* be put (in the "Letter on Humanism"): "Man is the shepherd of Being." But it would be too sharp a reduction to ascribe to this "folksy" origin the broad role Heidegger assigns the Volk in his conceptual scheme—and this demurral would hold even if, as I have suggested, Heidegger offers no independent systematic ground for introducing the concept of the Volk or for his turn to the German Volk in particular.

On the one hand, then, Heidegger's reliance on the German Volk or (more generally and logically prior) on the Volk as such remains conceptually and empirically ungrounded—measured by the standards he himself applies to other thinkers. Certainly he provides no specific justification for according the Volk (in general or particular) an essential role in the disclosure of Being or Truth or as having a privileged position (and thus special obligations) in rescuing the modern world from the unhappy condition in which, repeatedly in his own history, Heidegger finds it. On the other hand, it is consistently through the mediating form of the Volk—perhaps not exclusively but persistently and even concurrently with such alternatives to it as art—that Heidegger asserts the possibility of the disclosure of Truth and Being, at least up to the point where pessimism about the possibility of such disclosure overtakes him. (And perhaps even then, since his bleakest predictions about the future of philosophy and thinking—in effect, about the future of the future—usually come with qualifications. Thus, even when he throws up his hands in despair in the *Spiegel* interview—"Only a god [or perhaps, 'another god': 'Nur noch ein Gott . . .'] can save us"—the implied plurality of gods suggests a sense of possibility that contrasts sharply with Nietzsche's proclamation of the *one* God's death, to which Heidegger himself often alluded.)

In the latter terms, then, even in the absence of arguments by Heidegger himself, we may still understand what it is in the structure of Heidegger's thinking that disposes it or finds a systematic need to insist on an at once philosophical and social role for the Volk. Heidegger's critique of the history of philosophy from the time of philosophy's fall after the pre-Socratics (Socrates himself, the "purest" of thinkers,[33] is included in this fall if he did not actually initiate it) was directed mainly at the subjectivization and developing nihilism he found in that history. Being and Truth receded there in the face of the development of increasingly distanced and technical criteria—including the now standard categories of epistemology and ontology and the principles of verification that replace Being and Truth with requirements established (in effect, *willed*) by philosophers themselves.

This conceptual apparatus that led in one historical offshoot to modern science is, however (on Heidegger's account), mistaken and harmful if understood, as it often has been, to represent thinking as such. Being and Truth "speak" only for themselves; they will not answer to criteria or requirements externally imposed. It is against the background of this objection that Heidegger, in the important essay of 1930, "On the Essence of Truth" (important enough for him to identify it as the beginning of the *Kehre* or "turn" that took him away from the project of *Being and Time*—although how far away that turn took him remains an issue), proposes a conception of truth as identical with freedom, designating the latter as "letting be." The standard correspondence theory of truth obscures this feature of Truth through its focus on the *criteria* of truth rather than on truth itself; by contrast, Truth as "letting be" enables beings to "reveal themselves with respect to what and how they are"; we find here the "disclosure of beings through which an openness essentially unfolds."[34]

For Heidegger it is crucial to distinguish the conception of freedom as "letting be" from the principle of tolerance or (as he would have it) "indifference" that is asserted in the liberal or bourgeois conception of freedom. (Heidegger's attacks on "bourgeois" values were no milder or less constant than Marx's—or, to be quite evenhanded, than his own attacks on Marx.)[35] Freedom understood as tolerance is for Heidegger among the notable and unhappy symptoms of modernity. Far from mediating between conflicting beliefs or truth claims, the exercise of freedom in these terms succeeds only in preserving discordant beliefs on the two sides without confronting whatever is in dispute: nothing changes. And the result of this analysis is as much to preserve error as to defeat it, in any event to represent truth itself as passive, a function—even when it becomes "known"—of human determination. Heidegger thus moves away from this view toward the opposing pole, and if his rejection of tolerance here does not commit him to an ideal of *in*tolerance, it removes one barrier that might stand in the latter's way.

The "letting be" that affords access to Being and Truth, by contrast, is active rather than passive, fostering engagement not with criteria interposed between the thinker and Being or Truth (criteria that must in turn require a ground in still others, and so on: Heidegger's hermeneutic version of the "third man" or infinite regress argument), but directly with Being and Truth as they disclose themselves. Heidegger's attack in the Rectoral Address on the tradition of "academic freedom" in the university on the grounds that this freedom expresses only a "lack of concern, arbitrariness in one's intentions and inclinations, lack of restraint in everything one does"[36] reapplies quite exactly his earlier and more general criticism of the concept of freedom as tolerance in "On the Essence of Truth." Maurice Blanchot emphasizes what he takes to be the very close relation between Heidegger's rectoral (and public) statements and his "philosophical" writing from even an earlier time (including *Being and Time*): "It is the same writing and very language by which, in a great moment in the history of thought, we had been made present at the loftiest questioning."[37]

From this point on Heidegger progressively emphasizes the definition of *aletheia* ("Truth") as an unveiling or disclosure—always with the stipulation, however, that the process will not occur without evocation and readiness. He thus hopes to avoid replacing the externally imposed epistemological categories of both realism and critical idealism with a subjectivist and (in his view) equally arbitrary version of intuition. There must then be mediation in *some* sense between Truth and its "finder," but mediation that demands no more of Truth or its knower than an opening or evocation; the mediating form will not in any event depend for *its* realization on a structural feature (in either the "object" or the "subject"), since this again would define Truth as criteriological rather than as speaking in its own voice.[38]

In which of its forms can mediation serve in this role? Only a limited number of logical possibilities occur here, and most can be quickly excluded. Notwithstanding the emphasis in phenomenology on categories drawn from individual experience, for Heidegger to rely on the individual *subject* as the agent of disclosure for Being would leave that process fragmented beyond repair (and before that, at odds with the "In-der-Welt-Sein" underlying phenomenology's critique of the subject-object distinction). In any event, no subsequent appeal to time or history could reconstitute the subject if it were dismembered in this way. On the other hand, to posit a common human faculty such as reason or understanding would be to relapse into the false objectification or scientism—one or another version of foundationalism—that had progressively driven philosophy in its modern history from its original and truer path. If Being and Truth are to be disclosed, then, it must be through an agency that mirrors their own involuntary or "natural" expressive character without at the same time becoming the passive and neutral, hence indifferent, medium that realist metaphysics had typically posited. (Passive, that is, in the conception of the medium—as in the "mirror of nature"—not necessarily in what the medium claims for itself; in such terms, even the motion of Aristotle's "active intellect" would be not quite active enough.)

It is at this systematic juncture in his thought that Heidegger introduces the concept of the Volk—at times of the Volk as such, elsewhere of a particular Volk, principally (again) the German Volk. This turn is not always explicitly noted, and as I have claimed, it is never fully grounded systematically; but it recurs in his work persistently and in a sufficient variety of contexts to be significant, appearing also in *Being and Time*, notwithstanding that work's emphasis on Dasein (*individual* existence) and its related features of "authenticity." To be sure, nothing in *Being and Time* that points in the direction of social mediation—like the concepts of "care" (*Sorge*) or of historicality—comes close to the emphasis in Heidegger's public statement made only a few years later, during his rectorate, that "the individual himself counts for nothing. It is the destiny of our people incarnated in its state that matters."[39] The latter is, however, more than just consistent with the earlier, philosophical work—although even if it were *only* consistent with it, this too would be telling.

If one asks by what process Heidegger arrives at the philosophically grounded assignment he conceives for the Volk—which is again not simply a biological or political or social entity but metaphysical—the genealogy that can be reconstructed by reading backward from his conclusions nonetheless seems clear. The goal of disclosure, of "thinking" Being or Truth, can be realized only through a means particular enough to represent individual thinkers and their thought, yet general enough to reach Being as such, not in its aspects or elements. Thus in his book on Nietzsche, where he decries the (then) present lack of any such mediating form (in some measure, in his view, a consequence of Nietzsche's own assaults on the past), Heidegger makes it clear what would serve this function:

> There is no longer any goal in and through which all the forces of the historical existence of peoples can cohere and in the direction of which they can develop; no goal of such a kind . . . that it can by virtue of its power conduct Dasein to its realm in a unified way and bring it to creative evolution. . . . Implied in the essence of a creative establishment of [such] goals . . . is that it comes to exist and swings into action, as historical, only in the unity of the fully historical Dasein of men in the form of particular nations.[40]

It should not be assumed that the concern for such mediation is initially motivated either by Heidegger's venture into politics or by his reaction to the results of that venture and their impact on his thinking. The ground, as I have suggested, is already present in *Being and Time* (1927), closely tied to the central concepts there of Dasein and "historicality." The "existential analytic" of Dasein not only rejects any merely "psychological or anthropological" account of the self, it also rejects the conception of the *individually constituted* self ("A bare subject without a world never 'is' . . . and so in the end an isolated 'I' without Others is just as far from being proximally given."[41] "By 'Others' we do not mean everyone else but me—those over against whom the 'I' stands out. They are rather those from whom, for the most part, one does *not* distinguish oneself.")[42] Or again, as Heidegger in the somewhat later (1936–38) but only recently published *Beiträge zur Philosophie* (*Contributions to Philosophy*) stresses the collective character of the Volk's expression: "The essence of the Volk is its voice. This voice, however, does not occur as an 'immediate' expression of the common, natural, moderated, and uninformed 'person.'"[43]

This synchronic condition of collectivity, furthermore, is reinforced diachronically—by Dasein's "authentically" historical character that extends to "the very depths of its Being": "When . . . one's existence is inauthentically historical, it is loaded down with the legacy of a 'past' that has become more recognizable, and it seeks the modern. But when historicality is authentic, it understands history as the 'recurrence' of the possible and knows that [such] possibility will recur only if existence is open for it . . . in resolute repetition."[44] Thus, whatever else inspires the projects of Dasein—the individual existent—it is bound by social and historical conditions defined corporately both horizontally (in relation to other beings) and vertically (in relation to the past and future). The terms, if not the title, of the Volk—or of some other Volklike expression—are in these respects anticipated.[45] For though the conditions cited *need* not be conceived corporately, that would be their most obvious and accessible formulation.

A quite different account of the role that Heidegger assigns to the Volk—and then to the German Volk and subsequently to Nazism—has traced it to "the absolute formalism of his philosophy of decision, in which the decision in itself is the greatest virtue."[46] On this account (the particular formulation by Hans Jonas is one of many), Heidegger's deferral to the Volk is arbitrary, since he provides no basis either for any particular form of mediation or for mediation as such. In other words, there is nothing in his systematic thought to prevent Heidegger's turn to the Volk (or to the German Volk or to Nazism), but neither would anything impel him toward one of those mediating terms more than toward some other one that was directly opposed. (This claim is distinct from that which represents the ideology of Nazism as so amorphous that virtually any assertion could be consistently attached to it.)[47] On this account, Heidegger could equally readily and consistently have introduced a quite different version of the mediating entity, like the democratic state—or even an altogether nonpolitical or extrapolitical structure. But both the latter alternatives are ruled out, I have argued—if not explicitly, by systematic premises in the foundation of Heidegger's thought, however remote these seem from demarcating a *political* position at all.

This conclusion is the point, I take it, of Karsten Harries's assertion that "once we recognize that authenticity demands the subordination of the individual to a common destiny, it becomes impossible to see the Rektoratsrede as diametrically opposed to *Being and Time*."[48] Once again the claim here is for something more than only consistency. No doubt, at some juncture in his conception of the relation between thinking and practice, decisions, for Heidegger, must make provision for their own warrant (at least decisions *require* a warrant). But however underdetermined his appeal to the Volk is as a basis for internal causality, one can still find in the former an element of the latter. The "philosophy of decision" that Jonas refers to, so far as it has a claim at all, thus becomes systematically relevant only later—when Heidegger himself decides to privilege a particular Volk.

Again, I have not been claiming that Heidegger's turn to the mediating form of the Volk—still more to the German Volk—is systematically *entailed*. But to impose a requirement of necessary connection or implication between the levels or branches or elements of philosophical systems would ensure the failure of virtually all such systems, including the most complex or historically important among them.[49] The relevant standard here should rather be—and constantly *has been*—one of disposition or probability in respect to positions or claims that the system either excludes or includes. In this sense the minimal claim for Heidegger's conception of the Volk—that it is not inconsistent with other systematic elements of his thinking—or beyond this, that it is likelier or more probable than other alternatives, claims a good deal. *Must* Heidegger invoke this mediating form or indeed any such form? No, but there is little among the levels of almost any philosophical system that would meet such a requirement. Would he not be more consistent by holding strictly to a contingent nominalism—a more authentic existentialism—from which he clearly seems here to depart? Perhaps, but consistent with only one side of the emphasis in *Being and Time*, which would then strain *another* emphasis that is hardly less significant there. Could there be other corporate mediating forms than the Volk that would serve the function indicated? Yes, but the differences among such mediating forms (e.g., the difference between the diffuseness, even the contradictory impulses in a pluralist democracy and the unity of purpose or consciousness ascribed to a "people") can also be measured by what the mediation is supposed to accomplish. Are there, then, grounds beyond the negative test of avoiding inconsistency for Heidegger's appeal to the conception of the Volk as a mediating form? That indeed is the claim asserted here.

The internal structure of Heidegger's thought in relation to the topics addressed thus includes the following elements: (1) he did not base his ontic/ontological claims, even in *Being and Time* and more clearly in his later works, on the primacy or independence of the individual subject; (2) no grounds systematically established in his work would entail that primacy or independence; and (3) to deny some form of mediation through a corporate structure extending beyond the individual agent or moment would be to contradict the concepts of time and historicity (and of individual human action) that, from *Being and Time* on, were fundamental themes of Heidegger's thought. How important the systematic role of this mediation is becomes evident in a statement in the *Beiträge zur Philosophie*: "[The] uppermost rung of Being will be attained if a *Völkisch* principle, as something determinative, is mastered and brought into play for historical Dasein."[50] The emphasis on corporate mediation is so marked here that even the historical character of the likely corporate forms diminishes in favor of their unified and more abstract "essences"; indeed, the *particularity* of individual historical actions or events seems in these terms to have less chance to assert itself.

Arguing from a different direction but also toward a finding of Heidegger's subordination of the particular or individual, both Jürgen Habermas and Richard Bernstein, in their respective analyses of Heidegger's political and moral thought, stress the obscuring of history fostered by his will for abstraction. So Habermas writes: "Concrete history remained for him a mere 'ontical' happening, social contexts of life a demonstration of the inauthentic. . . . If his tale of an 'essential happening' had any meaning at all, the singular event of the attempted annihilation of the Jews would have drawn the philosopher's attention."[51] And Bernstein, reflecting on Heidegger's willingness in the Bremen lectures to "dismiss the difference between motorized agriculture and mass murder as 'non-essential,'" concludes that "it is as if in Heidegger's obsession with man's estrangement from Being, nothing else counts as essential or true except pondering one's [collective] ethos."[52] Both Habermas and Bernstein thus criticize Heidegger for having ignored the need—more basically, the *fact*—of historical or social mediation in favor of a more abstract and ahistorical process. I have been arguing to the contrary—that Heidegger *did*, through the concept of the Volk, acknowledge and indeed confront that need, but that he did this in terms so far abstracted from history as to subvert his own purpose (at least one part of that purpose)—in order, one supposes, to leave the voice or mediator of Being as uncontaminated by history as was Being itself. It is, then, the failure of his *effort*, not the failure *to make it*, that mars his thinking on the issue, making it a thoughtful failure rather than simply one of omission.

This conception of the role of a Volk and then, more specifically, of the German Volk in invidious comparison with others means that there would be—*could* be—little to say about those other "peoples" for whom satisfying the requirement of a metaphysical "essence" (beyond the common adherence to a language or a land, but including them) was in doubt. Certainly Heidegger recognizes the *existence* of other peoples: he speaks repeatedly of the (ancient) Greeks, less often of the Romans (and disparagingly, insofar as as he finds Greek texts contaminated and skewed by the Latin), the French, the Russians—but still in terms that only rehearse features more definitively present in the German Volk. But no more in describing the latter than the former does he provide a conceptual or empirical analysis of the systematic place he reserves for the Volk; that is, for justifying his ascription of an "essence" to such entities. Indeed, the question whether that kind of analysis would be pertinent, let alone required, does not arise for him. And if we can understand why Heidegger might choose to avoid equating "Volkhood" with individual historical features like political autonomy or the possession of a physical homeland (although each of these has *some* role in his thinking about the Volk and in his denial of the Jewish Question), Heidegger proposes nothing in lieu of them that singly or together locates the Volk as a historical—in contrast to a metaphysical—entity.

In systematic terms, the general concept of the Volk then becomes an axiom in his systematic thought, first motivated by systematic needs and then refined by a second-level stipulation that goes on to privilege the German Volk. If there is a systematic ground at least of probability, as I have argued, for the first of these steps, neither early nor late in his work does any appear for the second. Beyond the latter stipulation on one side, furthermore, and Being and Truth on the other, little space remains for other individual "Völker" even if one were willing to concede the abstract principle of the "Volk" in general. The principle is to that extent a "form" without instantiation—until, that is, the German Volk is identified as its exemplar. Other peoples do not count, not because they have been tried and found wanting, but because the criteria of "Volkhood" that are then brought to a point in the German Volk exclude other peoples even before they can be tried. Disputing this claim, Michael Zimmerman has argued both that the concept of the Volk leaves room in principle for a plurality of "peoples'" voices and thus destinies, and that this plurality is a significant aspect of Heidegger's intention for the concept.[53] A striking implication of this interpretation, however, would be that even if one granted Heidegger's own privileging of the voice of the German people and language, the voice of a different Volk might come to occupy the same position, might be entitled to make the same claims. But although statements to that effect could be made in the name of other nations *by them*, it is more than just unlikely that Heidegger would grant those others the same efficacy he grants Germany—and not only because of the logical inconsistency this would involve. Peoples might be "chosen" for different roles; it is difficult to see how different peoples could be (distinctively) chosen for the same role.

There was then no Jewish Question for Heidegger because no systematic question could be based on the existence or status of other peoples at all, whether in the modern or the premodern worlds. (His evocation of the Greeks remains as suspect systematically as his evocation of any other Volk.) To this extent Heidegger's silence on the Jewish Question was not invidious, since it extended beyond the Jews to other peoples as well. It becomes invidious, however, as sustained by the historical conditions of which Heidegger was part and could not have been unaware, yet which he would consistently deny, including first the presence and then the absence of Jews from the midst of the Volk of which Heidegger held himself a willing member. That in Heidegger's view it is the Germans who are "in fact" privileged would be only another, heightened reason for his denial and not only avoidance of the Jewish Question. There can be little doubt, in any event, that the historical disappearance of the Jewish Question—an occurrence no less evident than the prior *existence* of the Question had been—would have brought the latter into even sharper focus for anyone who, unlike Heidegger, had not thought and affirmed its denial.

Heidegger's silence is thus a silence preserved in the midst of a sea of words and sound which speaks as loudly as they do, denying the possibility of a presence to which a glance at history would have attested. And as a consequence of that silence, there can be little uncertainty or mystery about why, after the Holocaust—in the absence of a Jewish Question in its time—there would also be for him no "Jewish Question." There was nothing to talk about; so far as his thinking about the Holocaust was concerned, the Holocaust might as well not have occurred. This silence about the Jewish Question, furthermore, was part of a larger silence about his own method and conclusions in respect to the nature of the Volk as that nature came to a point in the German Volk, a conjunction of assertions embedded in his thought that he persistently refused to acknowledge or confront—to think. Prejudice there may have been as an attendant cause of this denial (I argue in the next chapter that there *was*), but Heidegger's silence is explicable without it.

Nor is the silence a consequence only of a practical error or misstep, as it would have been had it followed only from a mistaken prediction about how a particular group or individual (the National Socialists or Hitler) would act in the future—although this is indeed

Heidegger's benign explanation of his own history as one that, writ small, reflects the "mistaken" history of Nazism writ large. When Heidegger comments to Marcuse (20 January 1948) that "I expected from National Socialism a spiritual renewal of life in its entirety, a reconciliation of social antagonisms and a deliverance of Western Dasein from the dangers of Communism,"[54] he is speaking of hope to which he felt entitled at a time when the first concentration camps had been built in Germany, when racial laws with their official rationales had been "legally" promulgated and their enforcement begun, and when one consequence of that new set of legal regulations had been to drive virtually all his onetime Jewish colleagues and students out of the university. Even at the time of the vote by which he was elected rector—"unanimously," as he misrepresented it in his 1945 statement "Facts and Thoughts"—thirteen out of ninety-three members of the Freiburg Senate had, on racial grounds, been declared ineligible to vote.

Heidegger's contention that National Socialism differed in its essence or spirit or principles from what the Third Reich turned it into is a recurrent theme in his post-Holocaust reflections. With that contention, he proposes to absolve himself of responsibility concerning his own Nazi affiliation except insofar as it involved a mistaken prediction about the course Nazism would take (and perhaps, as having misjudged the extent to which he himself might be able to influence that course). Whatever fault there was, then, was not even the fault of ignorance—since in predictions about the future no one has the privilege, let alone the assurance, of knowledge. Heidegger's mistake in this connection too would have thus been "only human"—a qualification he elsewhere attaches to a mistake he does acknowledge; but to the extent that it was "only human," of course, it hardly counts as a mistake at all. The most that can be required of anyone who gambles morally on the future—as everyone does and has to—is a *reasonable* expectation; after that, even predictions that fail are morally innocent.

To be sure, when Heidegger first informally and then formally associated himself with the designs of National Socialism, he based those commitments on evidence that looked forward to a still contingent future. There is, moreover, an obvious difference between viewing an event in prospect, when it is still unfolding, and the retrospective view of that same event after history has excluded other possibilities. Thus if the turn Heidegger took was a misstep in the way that a morally steady walker may sometimes trip, one might challenge Heidegger's silence on the Jewish Question and yet find that silence incidental to his more basic project; it would thus be an error that anyone might have made and indeed that many others did make. In fact, however, that "misstep" was integral to the project he had defined for himself and for philosophy. It followed, furthermore, from his earlier acceptance of the grounds on which that choice (of post-Holocaust silence) was made: from a time when the Jewish Question still was—and was yet also then answered by him with silence. Also that silence, I have been claiming, was not one of indifference or inattention, but of his own doing. That is, of his thinking.

CHAPTER FOUR

Inside and Outside
Heidegger's Antisemitism

The thinking of the philosopher . . . has always so much world-space to spare that in it each thing—a tree, a mountain, a house, the cry of a bird—loses all indifference and commonplaceness.

Martin Heidegger, *An Introduction to Metaphysics*

F OR HEIDEGGER, then, there was no Jewish Question and subsequently would be no "Jewish Question." In this sense, with both those questions suffused by silence, there would be for him no line demarcating the two—no difference, that is, between the pre- and post-Holocaust periods. And if the chain of moral causality held here to be responsible for this sequence of denial—grounded in Heidegger's evocation of Being and Truth through the privileged access of the German Volk—seems too large for its alleged effect, this conclusion may reflect only an underestimate of the effect's significance. In any event, the factors in the proportion are unavoidable in any account of Heidegger's thought; whatever else might be added or subtracted, Heidegger's common denial of both the Question and the "Question" stands firm, insistently calling attention to itself. Yet the lineage of this denial would remain incomplete without reference to one other factor that, although it does not materially alter the thesis so far posited here, is relevant to it. This consideration may appear "merely" biographical or anecdotal, and indeed—*systematically*—that is what it amounts to. In its own right, however, it stirs impatiently beside both the Question and the "Question," shaping another question that, without displacing the first two, demands a space of its own: the question, that is, of whether Heidegger was an antisemite.

The apparent conciseness of *this* question is misleading, in part because by itself the answer to it may be little more informative if it is yes than if it is no. Substitute a variety of other names for Heidegger's, and the layers of assumption and ambiguity in the question become evident, beginning with the designation of "antisemitism" itself. That term, we know, was intended by its principal initiator, Wilhelm Marr, as a *racial* rather than a religious or cultural characterization, with Marr insistent that it represented a scientific distinction, that it was not an expression of religious prejudice or even reference. The Jews as a race, in his view, possessed certain biological characteristics whose consequences posed a social menace.[1] This coinage anchors the term's meaning in a premise of biological racism that invidiously distinguishes the "Semites"; indeed, our own use of the word might be accused of reiterating this part of its original definition, although we also assume that its current denotation has been extended to cultural or social and in any event nongenetic referents. Nonetheless, the term's origins continue to reverberate, and just because of this, alternative locutions have been proposed for "antisemitism" that do not carry its historical presuppositions.[2] These revisions, it should be noted, come from all directions; Goebbels, for example, initiated a Nazi ban on the use of the term, certainly not out of opposition to the practice and not because he thought the concept had no scientific basis, but because its referent was too broad: the menace of the Jews was due not to their racial character as Semites but to their more specific identity, *among* the Semites, as Jews.[3]

This, however, is only the first in a series of problems related to the concept and not only the term "antisemitism." Thus, for example, the issue of proportionality: Is the same category to apply equally to conduct that on one side involves verbal slurs ("to 'jew' down the price of something") or social exclusion from a club—

and that on the other side is responsible for *genocide*? Or again: Marr and his followers identified themselves as antisemites. This self-description should count for something even if, like other self-descriptions, it is not necessarily decisive. Admittedly, it would be unusual to find someone who described himself as antisemitic but who wasn't in fact, although the converse of this is relatively common: many people who reject the characterization ought nonetheless to be designated by it. (To be sure, few statements reflect this dissonance as forthrightly as that of the English diplomat and writer Harold Nicolson: "Although I loathe anti-Semitism, I do dislike Jews.")[4]

Yet instances also occur where it is understandably difficult to decide whether to affirm or deny the reference. So, for example, the principled Kant, writing well before Marr coined the term (and as ever, one supposes, on behalf of Enlightenment), offhandedly characterizes the Jews as "a nation of cheats," so thoroughly inclined to that role that any attempt to make them "moral in regard to deceit and honesty" would be "pointless."[5] Does that in itself make Kant an antisemite? And if it does, are we bound to apply the same term—intending the same meaning—to Hitler? Adolf Eichmann claimed to have acted only under orders in organizing the deportation of hundreds of thousands of Jews to the death camps, insisting at his trial in Jerusalem that he himself had "nothing personal" against Jews: if we can imagine taking Eichmann at his word (obviously at odds with many of Hitler's), would "antisemitism" in the same sense fit here as well? The issue thus raised comes from opposite sides: What, minimally, justifies the charge of antisemitism? And what, maximally, pushes antisemitism beyond the limits of that concept into another, larger one? And then—to the immediate point—where does Heidegger stand on this spectrum?

I have already cited a number of statements in which Heidegger claims evidence in his own writing of his objection to the biological racism asserted in Nazi orthodoxy. From the contexts in which these retrospective appeals appear, it is clear that his intention in proposing them is to defend himself against the charge of antisemitism; to demonstrate, by showing that he was not and had not been a biological racist, that whatever else follows from his association with National Socialism, it would be wrong to hold him accountable (even in principle) for the Nazis' anti-Jewish policies or, still worse, for the practices that resulted from those policies. In other words, for Heidegger the concept of antisemitism *entails* a commitment to biological racism; since he rejects the latter—presumably because of the inadequacy of its scientific claims—he judges himself innocent on the charge of antisemitism.[6] (Whether or not the passages he cites from his own earlier work demonstrate this opposition to biological racism, he clearly means to reject that view at the time he interprets his own earlier statements.)

That Heidegger was not a racist on biological grounds—or more generally, a biological or any other kind of determinist—will, however, surprise no one familiar with his work, early or late. Whatever it is in Dasein or any other central feature of the human project that defies mechanistic or, for that matter, rationalist determination, Heidegger's emphasis on that rejection is clear. "The contexts of assignments or references which, as significance, is constitutive for worldhood, can be taken formally in the sense of a system of Relations. [A contrasting] . . . kind of Being gives us an *existential* way of determining the nature of Being-in-the-world, that is, of Dasein."[7] Accordingly, however Dasein makes its way in the world, it will not be, reductively, as a product of its past conditions or relations in that world.

But to acknowledge this distinction is not to resolve the issue of its application to antisemitism, specifically as Heidegger assumes the *biological* ground (in its Nazi formulation or some other) to be a necessary condition for antisemitism or racism as such. For in sharp contrast to that view, one can point to varieties of pre-Mendelian antisemitism that do not depend on biological or genetic premises at all—as well as to instances of post-Mendelian antisemitism that, even when they appear in association with biological theories, are conceptually independent of them. The stereotyping and psychological determinism that are common features of racist and antisemitic discourse have been articulated no less readily—and arguably more seriously—in cultural or metaphysical terms than in biological ones. And it is difficult to understand how Heidegger would have been unaware of these alternatives or why it would have seemed self-evident to him, as it apparently did, that what was objectionable or even contestable in the rationale for racism would turn exclusively on its biological claims; that is, on whether those putatively scientific claims could stand up as science.

The effect of Heidegger's narrowly defined conception of antisemitism is, again, to leave untouched a range of other cultural or social—or metaphysical—sources on which racism (and more narrowly, antisemitism) has continually drawn. Given the far-ranging consequences that follow from it, one can only speculate about the explanation for this invidious distinction in his thinking. One possible explanation, of course, is that in its cultural or social or metaphysical varieties, antisemitism did not seem to Heidegger wrongful or prejudiced at all; that in *those* forms, he viewed antisemitism not as racism but (as many others held then and continue to hold) as a warranted cultural response to the evidence of European social history and more generally, for him, to the history of Being. The sense of this possibility is much sharper in Heidegger's scientific-sounding claims about *blacks*: "in common with minerals . . . neither [of them] think."[8] The latter claim so obviously does impinge on biological grounds that if one accepts Heidegger's insistent rejection of biological racism, one would have to conclude that he regards blacks as sufficiently remote from human categories not to qualify as a (human) race at all (a fortiori, not to qualify for Volkhood).

The pressure for an explanation of this sort is increased by the fact that biological racism, in its Nazi version or any other, is arguably impossible to sustain in conceptually coherent terms—a consideration that figured in the confusions of the Nazi analysis of race itself. The issues of the definition of "race," for example, and then of how to apply that category have proved intractable against the considerable efforts made to advance that thinking in both the natural and the social sciences. Certainly there is nothing close to a consensus on the biological definition (or number) of races even among those who find the concept useful—and if, after a century's search for evidence and conceptualization, disagreement can in-

clude categorical denials like the statement of the mainstream bi-
ologist Stephen Jay Gould that "I reject a racial classification of hu-
mans,"[9] it seems reasonable to conclude that an intrinsic problem
affects the concept and, by implication, also the supposed phenomenon.

Still more compelling evidence of this internal confusion is apparent in the arbitrariness (in other contexts the result would have
been embarrassment) of attempts to base social policy on racial
and biological distinctions. This flaw is evident in the history of
Nazi racial legislation itself. So, for example, the first formally biological specification of Jewish identity by the Nazis that appeared
in the *Arierparagraph* shortly after the Nazis' assumption of power
in early 1933 stipulated that one Jewish grandparent would suffice
for that racial designation to be transmitted; by 1935, when the
"Nuremberg Laws" were promulgated, this condition of identity
was narrowed to a requirement of *three* Jewish grandparents. (Both
regulations also identified other sufficient conditions, but each included the one sufficient "biological" ground.) Quite aside from
the arbitrariness of their differences, both formulations begged the
question of what biological evidence determined the "Jewish" status of the grandparents (however many there were required to be).
And quite aside also from this methodological problem, it was obvious even at the time that the shift to the second, more restricted
definition was due rather to prudential than to biological concerns.
Put simply, the first definition would have included too many as-
similated "Germans" with one Jewish grandparent, who would
thus be identified and then have to be confronted as Jews. Yet *some*
criterion had to be established if anti-Jewish regulations were to be
possible at all. Reports of the chaotic last-minute scramble to come
up with a set of racial criteria in time to announce the "laws" before the Nuremberg Rally ended (15 September 1935) would, in almost any other context, qualify as farce.[10]

These conflicting pressures were never far from the consciousness of Nazi ideologues, and awareness of the conceptual difficulty that fostered them—together with the refusal to admit
embarrassment in the face of it—predated the Nazi regime. Early
in the immediate background of Nazi antisemitism, for example,

the difficulties of defining Jewish racial identity (certainly more an acknowledgment of the difficulties than a solution for them) were graphically summarized in the exasperated declaration of the popularly antisemitic mayor of Vienna, Karl Lueger: "Wer Jude ist, 'bestimme ich" ("Who is a Jew, *I* decide"). On this crucial matter of the criterion of identification, the "one drop" rule of American racial definition of blacks—according to which a single "drop" of "black blood," infused from no matter how many generations past, establishes black identity—at least has consistency on its side,[11] though faced with the same substantive difficulties.

Admittedly, the conceptual incoherence of biologically based racism (and so of biological antisemitism) does not mean the doctrine could not win adherents. What is entailed, however, is that notwithstanding the exemption that a denial of biological racism might bring from one important strand of "normative" Nazi racism, it would not by itself dispel the charge of antisemitism *as such*, since that charge could consistently refer to *other* elements motivating Nazi antisemitism as well as earlier forms.[12] It is obvious that the history of antisemitism antedates not only Marr's formulation of the term but also biological racism more generally. Certainly there are manifestations of antisemitism from before the Christian Era to the present that in other of their features (stereotyping, scapegoating, even certain "remedies" prescribed for "solving" the Jewish Question) closely resemble racial antisemitism *except* for the biological determinant. To deny "antisemitism" as an explanatory or causal factor in the Jewish expulsion from Spain or the Inquisition or in the writings of a Luther or a Voltaire because the modern concept of biological determinism is missing from them imposes a distinction that the differences among them fail to support.[13]

Conversely, there is no reason to assume that antisemitism minus the factor of biological determinism occurs only before the development of nineteenth-century biology and genetics. Much twentieth-century antisemitism, *including* much of its expression in Nazi sources, cites justifications that are conceptually and practically independent of biological factors. Little of the cultural, social, and economic invective found in modern antisemitic writings—

ranging in the substance of their charges from accusations of dishonest business practices to divided national loyalties to the "blood libel"—logically presupposes or entails a genetic or biological ground in the Jews. That these charges are sometimes associated with biological causes is not incidental, but neither is it necessary. (Even the recurrent biological metaphors by which the Nazis refer to the Jews—with the Jews called "bacilli" or "cancers"—have a figurative force distinguishable from their literal denotation.)[14]

In the end, then, the question whether Heidegger was antisemitic cannot be decided on the grounds of his own disclaimers, and surely not by his contention that since biological racism is a condition of antisemitism and he is not a biological racist, he is therefore exonerated. The *metaphysical* racism indicated by Heidegger's view of the German Volk provides a basis for at least one alternative version of antisemitism that goes not only beyond personal prejudice but beyond psychological or social categories more generally. (Heidegger himself is sufficiently conscious of this distinction to cite Nietzsche's precedent in rejecting "biological" racism in favor of "metaphysical" racism[15]—a precedent, incidentally, that Heidegger found congenially elaborated in Mussolini and Hitler.)[16] A more specific counterpart or application of metaphysical racism appears in "metaphysical antisemitism" (or in Dieter Thoma's illuminating and harsher term, "*a*-semitism"),[17] where the animus against the Jews reflects an invidious distinction between a Jewish "essence" or "spirit" and the "essences" or "spirits" of other people(s).

Admittedly, the charge of Heidegger's antisemitism must face counterevidence registered both by Heidegger and by a number of commentators; this consists mainly of accounts of (allegedly) cordial associations Heidegger maintained with certain Jewish students and colleagues not only before but during the Nazi period.[18] But the basis for such counterclaims is equivocal, both in their own terms and in respect to other evidence they do not address. Under the latter heading, for example, come a number of otherwise unexplained *breaches* in Heidegger's relations with Jewish and non-Jewish but liberal colleagues and students during the Nazi period.[19] And still more basic than counting instances on the two sides of this line, there remains the question of the relation between antisemitism articulated in principle and antisemitism in its practice—with a range of variation, including exceptions, among the latter that does not nullify the principle.

For someone to maintain close relations with individual Jews does not itself refute or contradict the charge of antisemitism—any more than philosemitism would be contradicted by an antipathy to certain individual Jews. The cliché "some of my [his, her] best friends are Jews" has become a set piece of hypocrisy and a subject for satire just because of its blindness to the compatibility between what it asserts and a thoroughgoing antisemitic predisposition. Few "moral" principles are not stretched at times to accommodate exceptions on personal or individual grounds—and the shakier the principle's conceptual base (notably in the case of antisemitism), the more common such exceptions are likely to be. Heinrich Himmler himself offered a sharply ironic version of the "Some of my best friends are Jews" formula in his complaint about the obstacles the Nazis had met (among *Germans*) in implementing the "Final Solution": "And then they all come along, the 80 million worthy Germans. Each has his one decent Jew. Of course the others are swine, but this one, his is first rate."[20]

Of course, if *other* evidence supplements the existence of the "best friends" who are Jews (and in the absence of counterevidence), the charge of antisemitism would be proportionately discredited. But such conditions do not apply to Heidegger, as can be seen from testimony that falls into several of the categories of evidence mentioned in the previous chapters. Once more we begin from Heidegger's own statements, moving to reports of statements he allegedly made, then to impressions reported *of* Heidegger—and last (more important here than before) to the evidence of what he did not say.

Also here the balance of explicitly antisemitic statements is slim; that is, in the number of pejorative references to individual Jews, or in references to Jews as a group that are attached to a pernicious stereotype. Slim but not nonexistent. In the statement (referred to in chapter 3) that Heidegger as rector sent to the Führer of the faculty at Göttingen (Professor Vogel), with the purpose of undercutting a proposed appointment to the rank of professor there for his own onetime student Eduard Baumgarten, Heidegger writes:

> By family and spiritual attitudes, Dr. Baumgarten comes from that liberal-democratic circle of intellectuals gathered around Max Weber. During his time here, he was everything but a National Socialist. It surprises me that he is teaching at Göttingen. I cannot imagine on what academic basis he has earned his habilitation. After disappointing me, he became closely tied to the Jew [Eduard] Fränkel, who had been active at Göttingen and was later expelled. I suppose Baumgarten found some protection by this shift in affiliation.[21]

Baumgarten's association with "the Jew" Fränkel—evidently, on Heidegger's reckoning, nothing more than that descriptor is needed to identify him or to characterize him negatively—is understood also to impugn Baumgarten's qualifications; the same association explains why Baumgarten would have been "protected." Or again, Heidegger writes in the earlier of the two letters on Baumgarten, addressed to Victor Schwörer, dated 2 October 1929, *this one*, however, intended to obtain a stipendium for Baumgarten, who at that time represents part of the defense against the "Jewification" (*Verjudung*)—by others—of "our German spiritual life":

> May I say here more explicitly what I could say in my letter of reference only indirectly; . . . we confront a choice between again bringing to our German spiritual life authentic, foundational forces and educators—or of finally subjecting it to the growing Jewification in the broader or narrower sense. In light of this large goal I would be especially grateful if Mr. Baumgarten . . . could be helped by means of a stipendium.[22]

Heidegger does not say specifically what he means by the "broader" or "narrower" senses of "Jewification," but his use of those terms leaves little to the imagination. Certainly a likely interpretation would have the "narrower" sense refer to the physical presence and advancement of Jews in the professions (as in the university) and the "broader" sense to the diffusion of Jewish influence in the culture as a whole. Baumgarten himself, in the "Conversation" reported by David Luban that appears as an appendix to this volume, recalls Heidegger's response when Baumgarten asked the name of an admiring young man who had moments before engaged him in conversation: "Oh, some Jew," Heidegger's response came.

Additional statements by Heidegger as reported by second or third parties have already been mentioned: so his reference to the conspiratorial "international Jewish fraternity" in the conversation recounted by Jaspers. We note here as well evidence at a further remove, in the form of impressions by observers who report their own interpretations of the evidence—for example, the observation by Toni Cassirer (Ernst Cassirer's wife) on the stormy debate between Heidegger and Ernst Cassirer that took place at Davos (1929). The by then open philosophical disagreement between the two thinkers was in her view insufficient by itself to account for Heidegger's intense animosity to Cassirer (including a refusal to shake hands with him): "We were also not unaware of Heidegger's inclination to antisemitism."[23] In a letter of 4 May 1933, Husserl describes how "difficult" he found Heidegger's "breaking off relations with me (soon after his appointment [as rector]) and in recent years his increasingly strongly expressed antisemitism—even against his group of admiring Jewish students and in respect to the faculty."[24] In this same category may be included a statement by H. W. Petzet, a onetime student and later friend of Heidegger's (writing after Heidegger's death in a book intended to *defend* him): "If he found any sort of city life repugnant, and if everything about city life seemed strange to him, this was even more true of the world spirit of those Jewish circles that dominated the great cities of the West."[25] Again, such statements report impressions *of* Heidegger, not his own words, but the accounts from disparate sources of considerable authority cannot simply be dismissed.

It is significant, although still open to interpretation, that on all the occasions after the war when Heidegger was challenged on his views or actions in respect to antisemitism—in the range of its

Nazi manifestations or as bearing on his personal conduct—his response invariably focused on his relationships with specific Jewish students or colleagues, without addressing the issue of antisemitism as a general doctrine. (The single exception I have found is in his general—and proportionately unsettling—reply to Jaspers, cited above, p. 38.) It is, once more, as if Heidegger assumed that the evidence of certain individual pedagogical or collegial relationships would be all the proof needed for judging his disposition toward Jews and thus for refuting the charge of antisemitism (again a variation on the theme of "some of my best friends . . ."). That other manifestations of antisemitism—for example, his support of the Nazi Party when it was disenfranchising Jews and sending them to concentration camps—were compatible with his maintaining friendly personal relations with certain individual Jews was a possibility he not only took for granted but used as evidence for claiming his own distinctive conception of Nazism. Furthermore, from evidence *not* provided by Heidegger (e.g., the account of Max Müller), we learn that a number of otherwise unexplained breaches occurred in his own relationships with Jews and their non-Jewish supporters soon after the Nazis took power.[26] (It is unlikely that he could have forgotten these exceptions, but this issue bears on the separate issue of his credibility, not on his antisemitism.) For these several reasons and, more generally, because the difference between antisemitism at the level of principle and its individual exemplifications (or exemptions) seems so evident—if not quite *self*-evident—there is a basis here too to speak of a silence that is expressive, that takes the form of an answer.

The items of written evidence thus cited from Heidegger himself may seem sparse or impressionistic—insignificant, at any rate, given the thousands of pages he wrote in his lifetime. I acknowledged earlier, moreover, that "how much" evidence is necessary to warrant the charge of antisemitism is a difficult question because of the concept's breadth: however clear at the extremes, its applications are disputable at its center. But whatever their proportions, Heidegger's antisemitic words *are* clear at times. And at no point, even after being confronted for a second or (on occasion) a third time by those words as they refer directly or by implication to

Jews, did Heidegger take any of them back; at no point did he express regret for having said them (even his one acknowledgment, that he would not say "today," thirteen years later, something he had said before, does not do this). At no point did he make a general statement that would define his understanding and judgment of the common *non*biological antisemitic characterizations of Jews or of the policies—biological or not—to which those characterizations had led.

In the *Spiegel* interview, Heidegger cites in his own defense his effort while rector to save the positions of two Jewish faculty members at Freiburg whom he was at the time being pressed to dismiss. But the letter in which he mounted this "defense" sheds quite a different light on it than does Heidegger's own description. In that letter he argues for the usefulness of making exceptions to the law under which the two professors were to be dismissed (the law requiring the exclusion of Jewish faculty from the university): the exceptions sought would, he claims, both avert criticism from abroad and help maintain the international standing of German science. The two professors whose positions were threatened, furthermore, are "refined Jews of exemplary character." In the same "defense" he explicitly states that his request for an exemption for the professors should not be understood as contesting the "need to apply the law unconditionally in the reorganization of the public service."[27] Unless one interprets the latter statements as merely tactical—for which much other supporting evidence would be needed—the letter as a whole hardly expresses opposition to antisemitism, certainly not in principle and only problematically in act.

Again, measured by the extremities of the contemporary Nazi rhetoric, Heidegger's statements, even in sum, are mild. But it is pertinent in making such a judgment to recall that the context in which the statements appeared included other much stronger affirmations of Nazi doctrine that *in context* could reasonably be understood as related. And of course it also included not only other *statements* of Nazi doctrine but its practice: from early 1933 on, the construction in Germany of a network of concentration camps (two of them close to Heidegger's birthplace, Messkirch, which retained a strong hold on him); the removal from the university of

Jewish professors (later to affect also those Heidegger "defended," but even when he was doing *this* having already led to the exclusion of other faculty and students); the book burning by Freiburg students—on 10 May 1933, a day set for similar "ceremonies" across Germany—that Heidegger claims to have forbidden but that took place anyway (Ott claims that in Freiburg rain cut short the book burning, but evidently not the attempt);[28] the Nazi boycott of Jewish businesses; and the progressive disenfranchisement of Jewish "citizens." Heidegger spoke often and emphatically during his rectorship about the ideals of National Socialism and about the "battle" of the German people to retrieve and reassert its true identity—and the newspaper accounts of his public statements appeared side by side with news reports of these other events. Neither the sources and recorders of those stories nor their readers would have found reason in them to dissociate the two types. Quite the contrary, in fact, and understandably—since the "types" not only were consistent but reinforced each other. And Heidegger would have had to be obtuse or willfully blind not to have been aware of this.

So—for one large example—there may be no way of demonstrating how much credence to give Heidegger's own contention in the *Spiegel* interview that his emphasis on the term *Kampf* ("battle" or "struggle") in the last paragraphs of his Rectoral Address ("All capacities of will and thought . . . must be developed *through* battle, must be intensified *in* battle, and must remain preserved *as* battle") was intended as an allusion to the sort of metaphysical *polemos* that Heraclitus refers to (as in fragment 43). But for one thing, Heraclitus himself is not mentioned in the Rectoral Address—though Clausewitz is, in the sentence following the statement just quoted. But even if one concedes the Heraclitean allusion, would Heidegger have been unaware of the currency of the term *Kampf* in Nazi rhetoric generally or of its very specific appearance in Hitler's own *Mein Kampf* (1924–26), which was by 1933 a public "classic" in a way that the fragments of Heraclitus could not be expected to be, even for the partly academic audience to whom the Rectoral Address was presented? Would not the term's use in these more current contexts have predictably overridden any oblique or ironic evocation of Heraclitus? (Heidegger later claimed not to have read through *Mein Kampf*, but that does not bear one way or the other on his recognition of the title's currency or of the book's themes.) And then too, one supposes, Heraclitus would have still been absent when, five months later, Heidegger urged six hundred previously unemployed workers who had just been given work (and had been assembled in a university hall to listen to him) to recognize "how difficult" would be the *Kampf* "to reach and shape this new [German] reality." (That speech was published, it should be noted, in *Der Alemanne, Kampfblatt[!] der Nationalsozialisten Oberbandens.*)[29]

The few items of evidence in Heidegger's own words that explicitly speak against Jews, then, are but one part of the record. Those words—present or absent—have to be read in conjunction with other events and words (by him and by others) that at the time were in plain view—in *Heidegger's* plain view as well as his readers'. The ascription of antisemitism, like that of any dispositional characteristic, follows a process of inference from evidence of conduct and speech—including also, as the context warrants this, consideration of what is *not* done or said. The degrees of probability for proposed interpretations range from impossible to necessary, and if the breadth of that span complicates interpretation, at least it does not leave interpretation equally open *in principle* to all possibilities. When William Buckley, in a more recent political controversy in the United States, struggled for a formula by which to characterize certain statements made by Patrick Buchanan during the 1992 presidential election campaign, he arrived at the tortured conclusion that those statements "could not reasonably be interpreted as other than anti-semitic." Probably more, but surely nothing less than this can be said about Heidegger's statements and conduct. If, that is, antisemitism can be ascribed to any position short of the express design to commit genocide. (Maurice Blanchot directs a similarly oblique charge against Heidegger—"A kind of anti-Semitism was not alien to him [Heidegger]."—and then goes on to find in *that* source the explanation of Heidegger's post-Holocaust silence.)[30]

There can be little question that antisemitism was a more fundamental passion for other figures in Germany than for Heidegger and was expressed more blatantly by them. It has been persuasively argued, furthermore, that a majority of Germans were only "moderately" disposed toward antisemitism, and that this disposition was in any event not an overriding factor in their support of Nazism, even during the war itself.[31] How to understand this finding is complicated by the difficulty of identifying human motivation from self-description and also, of course, by the problem of measuring a "disposition" for antisemitism in particular or relating that disposition to its likely consequences. But whatever the difficulties of definition here, and however one judges the categories of "typical" or "moderation" in respect to Heidegger or more generally, the consequences of those categories make the charge of "extremism" seem irrelevant. And though a case can be made that in other notable contemporary intellectual and artistic figures even outside Germany antisemitism is more explicit and fully elaborated than in Heidegger (in T. S. Eliot, Ezra Pound, Louis-Ferdinand Celine), this difference may be less compelling than it might seem. Heidegger spoke and wrote from within the eye of the hurricane, with many other voices around him saying loudly and often what he himself could join—answer—by his own silence.[32]

Such instances of historical contextualization, then, do not refute or even mitigate the charge of antisemitism against Heidegger. That other academic figures in or outside public life were more extreme or explicit in their advocacy of Nazi doctrines, including antisemitism, does Heidegger no credit—any more than one would necessarily find moral *failure* in the fact that even as a non-Jew he did not simply leave Germany in solidarity against the advent of Nazism. (The account of Paul Tillich's decision to emigrate, in the face of official Nazi blandishments, offers a vivid contrast here.)[33] If the latter contrast was retroactively imposed as an obligation on Heidegger, it would perhaps demand too much; but by the same token, what he did do, judged by the criteria of "opposition," appears slight to the point of invisibility—and one reason for this is the evidence of his antisemitism.

In defending to Karl Löwith in 1936 his role and actions as university rector, Heidegger remarks that "things would have been much worse if at least a few intelligent people hadn't become involved. . . . If these [other] gentlemen hadn't been too refined to get involved, then everything would be different, but instead I'm entirely alone now."[34] We thus learn that already at *that* time, in the first years of its rule, National Socialism had swerved from the course that Heidegger had hoped and expected for it. This early theme becomes much enlarged in Heidegger's retrospective—post-Holocaust—comments, as he emphasizes the difference between what he believes Nazism could and should have been and what it in fact turned out to be.

Although Heidegger's reaction in these terms was intended to distinguish his own relation to National Socialism, the reaction itself was not distinctive but expressed a common point of view in Germany, especially in the early postwar period. (So, for example, a poll conducted by the United States military government from the end of the war to August 1946 showed that between 42 percent and 55 percent of the respondents "were convinced that National Socialism had been a good idea, but poorly implemented.")[35] The evidence also suggests that if Nazism *had* turned out as Heidegger hoped, antisemitism might well have been among its elements—not simply as a price to be paid for its advantages, but as integral to the transformation Nazism would effect. If there is no basis, direct or circumstantial, for attributing to Heidegger an explicit will or even assent to genocide, neither is there reason to regard the will to genocide as a necessary condition for characterizing the antisemite. And for a lesser but quite real variety of antisemitism—with the possibilities which, post-Holocaust, it opens to greater extremity—the combination of what Heidegger says and what he does not say, viewed against an unmistakable background, amounts to a substantial basis. At the very least it argues for a thoughtful indifference to the possibility of such extremity.

Doesn't the claim of Heidegger's antisemitism contradict the earlier assertion here—the central thesis of this discussion—that there was for Heidegger neither a Jewish Question nor a "Jewish Question"? Would not recognition of one or the other or both have been implicit within the bounds of his antisemitism? And since his antisemitism, as defined here, has been followed at least as far back as 1929 (it arguably extends further), would not that also mean the two questions were in their own times present and constant as well?[36]

But it is pertinent that I have not been arguing in this chapter for anything more than a psychological or social ground for Heidegger's antisemitism—insisting that even if such grounds can be disclosed (as I believe they have been), his denials of the Jewish Question and the "Jewish Question" do not depend on them, that those denials can and do stand on their own metaphysical feet. As an antisemite might nonetheless have Jewish friends, so the concept of the Volk underlying Heidegger's denial of the Jewish Question and the "Jewish Question" *need* not lead to antisemitism. Metaphysical racism does not entail any particular psychological or social prejudice, although it is admittedly improbable that *no* particular expression would follow from the principle. In this sense Heidegger's antisemitism is systematically independent of his stance on the Jewish Question or the "Jewish Question"—and the discussion here of his antisemitism is intended not to conflate his positions on the two matters but to emphasize that although they *in effect* reinforce each other, so far as his thinking goes they are conceptually independent.[37]

It may also be, then, that Heidegger was aware in cultural or psychological or sociological terms of the Jewish Question or the "Jewish Question." But in respect to his thinking, those questions are absent, silent—in effect denied, with the denial itself thoughtful, deliberate, meditated. About the "Jewish Question," the status of the Jews seen retrospectively through the Holocaust, there can be no doubt of his silence as a refusal, a denial; about the Jewish Question—the status of the Jews before the Holocaust—we have seen further evidence of exclusion or, more exactly, of *preclusion*: the Jews would not be permitted to pose, much less become, a question, since the conception of a Volk constituted their dismissal in prospect.

Admittedly, to assert or think a denial is at least to affirm the content of the negative proposition: Does not Heidegger *think* the Jewish Question (or "Jewish Question") at least this far? But if on the much-disputed boundary between epistemology and metaphysics we leave only *some* space for the "nothing" rejected in the classical Parmenidean or Platonic view (in the claim that all that can be said or thought about the nothing is only that it "isn't"), we find also these two instances of denial as deliberate rather than as mere prejudice or distaste. At the very least, the connection between personal inclination and theoretical affirmation discloses itself as weightier than only a psychological or even an epistemic issue.

And it is on this metaphysical boundary between inclination and thinking that Heidegger's cultural or psychological anti-semitism at once touches and remains distinct from his denial of the Jewish Question and the "Jewish Question." The two lines of address, then, remain systematically independent, although they reinforce each other in fact and even if, in considering the person in whom they both appear, the two converging lines may at times be impossible to distinguish (in contrast to other of Heidegger's clearly discernible features). But we can hardly insist as a *special* requirement that we be able here fully to distinguish particular strands of motivation for an act when we would not require this elsewhere.

What difference would it make—*against* the position I have been defending—if Heidegger's "personal" antisemitism was indeed the source for the causal chain in his thinking that led from his denial of the "Jewish Question" back to the denial of the Jewish Question? That difference would, I think, be decisive—for understanding Heidegger and also in its theoretical consequences. If his antisemitism was an expression only of personal taste, it would be distinguishable from his "serious" thinking; and if his antisemitism as a prejudice proved then to be tied to his political views more generally, that ensemble of public and personal dispositions would leave his professional—impersonal—thinking free of contamination from his personal dispositions even when that thinking took on the public face of politics. His "philosophy" would still have to answer for its own assertions, but it would not be responsible for acts or statements in Heidegger's "life" more directly linked to his psychological impulses and moods or to his social practices.

If Heidegger had been an engineer or a farmer or a tradesman, the distinction between his personal dispositions (then defined to include his politics, his religious views, and so also his *Weltanschauung* or "philosophy") and the products of his work would be assumed as a matter of course. Again, if like Degas he had gained recognition for the color and draftsmanship in his paintings of ballet dancers or horses, there would be no basis for introducing to the judgment of those paintings even the undisputed fact of his (nonpainterly) antisemitism. And if, as Richard Rorty puts it in his response to the question of the relation between Heidegger's Nazism and his philosophy, "being an original philosopher is like being an original mathematician . . . it is the result of some neural kink that occurs independently of other kinks,"[38] then the same conclusion would follow, and in still stronger terms. Heidegger's antisemitism—and the politics and other public conduct it might seem to be associated with, together with all his other tastes and perhaps even other modes of thinking—*should* be judged entirely apart from his "philosophical" work.

But this is, of course, precisely the claim I dispute here as not only not *self*-evident but contrary to what evidence there is. Even if we assume an emotive source or "thoughtlessness" in Heidegger's antisemitism (as in his formulaic reference to the "dangerous international fraternity of Jews" reported by Jaspers), there is no reason also to assume that his rendering of the Jewish Question and the "Jewish Question" comes only or mainly from that source—especially when we find at hand a conceptually more integral possibility in Heidegger's philosophical reflection, one that occupied him more constantly and deliberately than any other. In terms of causal origins alone, only a source of that kind, in contrast to something like antisemitic "prejudice" (and a fortiori, to a specifically antisemitic "neural kink") could explain the systematic connections and symmetry between his public and personal writings before, during, and after his rectorship and his philosophical or theoretical writings more narrowly defined.

It might be objected that *this* symmetry also is no more than accidental: that the several levels from which evidence for the symmetry is drawn are logically independent of each other. But it is difficult to see what more than has been provided could be required as evidence for a connection among these levels—short of demanding a systemwide logical entailment among them that few of the greatest philosophers have realized (or for that matter claimed). Hobbes is perhaps the one classical thinker of stature for whose work the connection between metaphysics and political or moral theory and practice might plausibly be construed as that of logical entailment (and for him too interpretations differ, with important readings disputing such metaphysical "reductionism").[39] In any event, the price this consistency exacts at each level of his mechanistic model—for the moment accepting the claim that he *achieves* the consistency—is high. Yet even critics like Hans Sluga, who object to Heidegger's public, political statements on historical and moral grounds, when they come to assess the systematic connection between the politics and the philosophy, still require just such an entailment relation between the two. In the absence of that connection, they conclude that the politics was based not on philosophical principle but on nonphilosophical disposition (and failure, though *that* then is quite a different matter). Or again, Kockelmans takes as crucial the question of an "intrinsic" (read "necessary") relation between Heidegger's philosophy, early or late, and Nazism; but because any claim for so strong a relation is "simply mistaken," the conclusion again follows that Heidegger's Nazism stands quite apart from his philosophical reflection.[40]

But surely such requirements of systematic entailment are stricter than what is typically demanded (or expected) even among the notable system builders in the history of philosophy whose works are nonetheless viewed as coherent wholes. If it were a condition for philosophical systems that they be formulated as (even covertly) deductive structures, they would look quite different than they do; at the very least, one would expect them to be translatable—and often translated—into deductive arguments by their readers, and even this has not been generally the case. (I am referring here not to the structure of particular arguments, but to the logical structure of the whole.)

On the other hand, that philosophical systems are not internally related deductively does not imply that their elements are related accidentally or arbitrarily, that each one of their claims answers only for itself. (The true—and perhaps only—genre of philosophical writing would on these terms be the "fragment.") Philosophy's history attests to a middle ground between those two alternatives,[41] where probability exceeds chance and falls short of necessity. This is the nature of the connection I have claimed between Heidegger's metaphysics as it invokes the concept of the Volk and, after that, concludes in his views on the Jewish Question and the "Jewish Question"—a concrete connection thus set against a background of more general and abstract relations. Heidegger's philosophical and "practical" writings and conduct were more than elaborations of merely personal antisemitic prejudice—which he also, in the event, had. On the other hand, from the personal to the abstract reaches of his thought, there *is* in his work a configuration that at once anticipates and represents his denials of both the "Jewish Question" and the Jewish Question—thus leaving a bequest of commonplace antisemitism without being dependent on it. It is in this sense that Heidegger was—is—both within and without antisemitism. Without it, insofar as his denials of the Jewish Question and the "Jewish Question" do not require or presuppose it; within it, since there remains a willing consistency between those denials and his antisemitism.

CHAPTER FIVE

Heidegger and the
Very Thought of Philosophy

Heidegger never thinks "about" something; he thinks something.

Hannah Arendt

I HAVE NOT CLAIMED that my discussion discloses new information about Heidegger's history or (with one exception, the Luban memoir) that it draws on material previously unpublished; I have also cited earlier accounts, as these bear on certain parts of the analysis. But as differences in perspective affect the representation and understanding of what is viewed, so to look at Heidegger "through" the Jewish Question sheds new light on the much discussed issue of his relation to Nazism as well as on the broader connection between his political stance and his "professional" philosophical thought. In part I sought the perspective of the Jewish Question (and "Jewish Question") on these matters precisely for one of the reasons it had previously been avoided: that as a starting point for philosophical thinking—and for thinking about that thinking—this perspective might appear parochial, a narrowly "Jewish" concern in comparison with other, putatively larger themes of Heidegger's thought within which the Jewish Question would seem to have a minuscule part if any at all. In the larger context understood in this way, moreover, the characterization of Heidegger as antisemitic would be of no greater philosophical interest, intrinsically *or* extrinsically, than his attitude toward any other group of people, his approach to more remote historical movements, patterns, or events, or even his more immediate and personal tastes. How much difference would it make for understanding or assessing his philosophical reflections to know what foods Heidegger especially liked or disliked?

The crucial point in the moral scrutiny of Heidegger, however, lies exactly at the juncture between these two undoubted sides of his life—in deciding exactly what belongs to its personal and subjective (even instinctual) side and what represents his systematically deliberated work. Certainly it begs the question to assume that political decisions or expressions, or "doing" more generally, are theoretically neutral or untouched just *because* they are practical. And again, it is the connection between these elements that I have asserted in considering Heidegger's relation to Nazism through the Jewish Question and the "Jewish Question" as these can be represented in his own philosophical terms. For it is not self-evident or (I have claimed) evident at all that Heidegger's political and public statements lacked theoretical significance in Heidegger's own understanding of them or in either the public or the philosophical reading that can be given them. His own statements point in fact to an integrating source for these two aspects of his work in what then appears as the unitary author: the person-philosopher.

To be sure, Heidegger's own work has sometimes been cited as anticipating postmodernist claims of the fragmentation of the once unified (now obsolete) subject; the individual self then appears as a series of contingent and dissociated moments of agency, divided so sharply that efforts at *re*construction must also be transparently partial and fragmentary. Connections discovered among such moments must then be either imposed externally or devised by the subject—in any event, created out of whole cloth and excluding any intrinsic or conceptual link between the theoretical and the practical. Heidegger himself, in the conversation with his onetime pupil Karl Löwith in Rome in 1936 (see above, p. 38), explicitly rejects this analysis of the relation between his public and professional expressions, insisting on the *connection* between the two. To maintain the distinction, then, would require that this assertion by Heidegger be written off as a mistake on his part—he *thought* he knew what he was doing but he didn't—or as an exception that proves the rule. (How many such exceptions would be required, one might ask, to disprove that rule?)

Heidegger himself—the public person standing beside the professional (or private) philosopher—thus appears as a test case of the very thesis of the subject's dissolution that has come to be associated with him. Arguments have been made and repeated that between his theory and his practice, between the public and the private moments of his life, between the professional philosopher and the amateur politico—in terms of the present discussion, between his view of the Jewish Question and his view of Being—there are no connections, certainly no *necessary* connections, and indeed none that are more than chance or incidental. The further conclusion is then drawn from this claim that the two sides of these dualisms must be assessed independently—which means, among other things, that Heidegger's stature as a philosopher can (more important, *ought* to) be judged, if not apart from history as such, apart from his own history, presumably including under that heading all but its most abstract or purest philosophical moments. The discussion of Heidegger here has argued to the contrary: that the verdict of a divided self, between Heidegger's political or public pronouncements and his philosophical work, is contradicted by the weight of evidence. And again, more specifically, that his denials of the Jewish Question and the "Jewish Question" that are by any account part of a larger "political" or moral stance are also much more than incidental to his nonpolitical—on some accounts this would be his *real*—thinking.

What implications does this conclusion have for the relation between the philosopher's life and thought as these have been, can be, distinguished—now referring by the former to acts or practices carried on without or even despite systematic reflection, following instinct or taste, or expressing the norms of a culture? I have suggested that where Heidegger is concerned this question has often been confused, by circular argument, with the question of the relation between his political views or conduct and his thinking, and I have hoped to show both that there *is* a difference between these two issues and that for him the connection between his politics and his "thinking" was systematically more basic than any distinctions that might be drawn between them. His denials of the "Jewish Question" and the Jewish Question turn out in the silence that ensues, then, to be neither inadvertent nor unmeditated; they too had been thought.

But what, then, of the other issue? Addressed in general: Are metaphysicians or, still more, writers on ethics—outside their texts—also obligated to be morally exemplary or even ordinarily "good"? Or addressed in particular, that is, in respect to Heidegger himself: What difference would—should—it make if we conclude (with Rorty, for example, a *philosophically* sympathetic reader) that Heidegger the person was indeed a "rather nasty piece of work— a coward and a liar pretty much from first to last"?[1] To be sure, Rorty intended his judgment to include Heidegger's political conduct and "thought," but the immediate issue here is not what features one includes in a definition of the philosopher's "person" but, however that is defined, what the relation is or ought to be between the person's moral character and that person's thought. The line between the alternatives here is sharp and unequivocal—and it is surely not irrelevant to that line or to Heidegger's philosophical standing in particular that contradictory views of this matter set out from a common view of him. So Gilbert Ryle offers a terse and categorical judgment of Heidegger the philosopher that would obviate the need for even a look at his work once a (negative) verdict was reached on his character: "Bad man. Can't be a good philosopher."[2] And from the other side, Hans-Georg Gadamer, a onetime student of Heidegger's who remained at once attached to and detached from him, offers an equally vivid assessment. Responding to George Steiner's puzzlement about the unlikely combination of Heidegger the thinker and Heidegger the man, Gadamer, reinscribing the distinction, found the solution "so simple": "[He] was the greatest of thinkers, but the smallest of men."

The hyperbole of Gadamer's assessment should not obscure the principle underlying it—that the philosopher as thinker and the day-to-day life lived aside from that (the separation is assumed) are indeed distinct—at most contingently, that is, occasionally, related. In the context cited, Gadamer does not direct his conclusion to what must be its severest test—the relation between an author's own conduct and the analyses to be found in his specifically ethical writings. But it is doubtful that even this case would change Gadamer's view of the principle he assumes, or that it detracts from what seems in comparison with Ryle's view the systematic and historical cogency of Gadamer's conclusion. Philosophers or their readers might wish it otherwise; they may well aspire to an ideal of the philosopher in whom thought and act are joined, for whom talk about virtue is linked to its practice, where the concept of the intellectual love of God becomes love indeed. But it seems indisputable that for many eminent figures in the history of philosophy, too little is known of their lives to provide historical assurance of any such links (for them or against them). And not only have philosophy's students or commentators thought it unnecessary to wait for evidence of such connections before asserting the philosophical importance of those figures, but it is difficult to imagine what evidence could be uncovered of venality in an Aristotle or an Augustine or a Hegel sufficient to affect their place in the history of philosophy. Indeed, where such evidence has been cited concerning the personal histories of philosophers—Rousseau, Marx, and Frege afford examples—the effect has been mainly that note is taken of the biographical information, which then simply appears side by side with the authors' respective doctrines and without prejudice to the latter. Certainly it would be difficult (more likely impossible) to demonstrate from the history of philosophy, as Ryle's contention implies, that significant philosophical accomplishment is in itself assurance of good moral character or conduct in its author.

To doubt this connection does not mean that philosophers may not be judged morally qua philosophers as well (independently) as persons apart from that role. But the evidence and judgment then articulated, in the first of these cases, are internal to the philosophers' work, not aspects of their biography. Philosophy can here look to both science and the arts for precedents: to the insistence of science that its conclusions speak only for themselves and to the judgment of which biography is irrelevant, and to art, where although the personal lives of creators are often introduced into critical narratives about their work, they provide no basis for assessing the latter's quality or importance or even, finally, their meaning. The distinction between artist and work, furthermore, extends as well to the relation between audience (or critic) and work. (So, for example, the theater director Charles Markowitz's summary judgment that "some of the most contemptible people I have ever known have loved Shakespeare.")

Again, whatever conclusion one reaches about the formal relation between philosophers' biographies and their work, that conclusion would not in any event undermine the difference between the issue of *that* relation and deciding whether a particular aspect of philosophers' conduct is to count as part of their "thought" or as an expression of personal taste about which there could be no disputing. Some of the evidence presented here evidently supports Rorty's characterization of Heidegger personally as a liar—and if one adds comments by other figures (such as Hannah Arendt)[3] who were in still better positions to know this, one might use such other terms as opportunistic, manipulative, hypocritical, vain, and self-indulgent. It may be, furthermore (though nobody yet claims evidence of *this*), that these traits are somehow related to aspects or implications of Heidegger's thought, perhaps including those evident in his denials of the Jewish Question and "Jewish Question." But it is important to recognize that even if such associations did occur, they and their consequences would have stood quite apart from the meditated denial of the Jewish Question and "Jewish Question" that has been the focus of discussion here. For on this account that denial—Heidegger's answer of silence—does not derive necessarily from his history or psychology or taste; rather, it stands on its own conceptual and philosophical—that is, extrabiographical—feet.

AGAIN, I HAVE MEANT to distinguish the relation between biography and philosophy for Heidegger from the relation between his politics and his philosophy—on the grounds of what I have held to be the systematic connection between the latter evident in his work. To be sure, that connection has been disputed, with counter-claims posed that extend to all the logical possibilities. Thus the two variables involved in the relation allow for four alternatives: (1) that Heidegger's political views and conduct were malign *and* that they were imbedded in his "deeper" philosophical work; (2) that his political views and conduct were malign but quite unre-lated to his authentic thinking; (3) that his political views and con-duct were benign—at worst, "honest mistakes"—*and* related to his philosophical thinking; and (4) that his political views and conduct were benign but were at any rate unrelated to his philosophical commitments.

Heidegger himself and his closest adherents (e.g., Jean Beaufret, Françoise Fedier) have defended the third of these accounts, argu-ing that the social critique implicated in Heidegger's pre-Holo-caust work, so far as there is one at all, is philosophically defensible (with this contextualization, his actions and statements in the role of rector at Freiburg become then, at worst, a conglom-erate human and honest mistake). The most radical contradiction of this view (committed to the first of the alternatives cited) is exemplifed in Theodor Adorno's summary condemnation of Heidegger's thought as "fascist right down to its innermost com-ponents."[4] Adorno thus finds not only consistency between Hei-degger's thought and his practice but a logical entailment; in these terms, Heidegger would have contradicted or betrayed his philo-sophical commitments had he *not* moved to his Nazi associations in practice. Rorty's view of the radical separation between Heideg-ger's politics (largely, though not entirely malign) and the signifi-cance of his philosophical work represents the second alternative; the interpretation of Heidegger as representing postmodernist irony and contingency ensures a sharp demurral from any *philo-sophically* totalitarian disposition on his part. It is difficult to find supporters of the fourth alternative, but since this would involve an apologia for Nazism without the benefit of even special plead-ing for Heidegger's version of it, that is hardly surprising.

There are, to be sure, shades and nuances within each of the sev-eral positions, most plentifully in the first. So, for example, Adorno asserts a necessary or intrinsic connection between the philosophy and the politics—but the claim can be made (as I have here) for a less strong but still more than accidental connection; thus the dispositional relation outlined in chapter 3, which in broad outline also resembles that proposed by such commentators as Luc Ferry and Alain Renaut, Tom Rockmore, and Michael Zimmerman. Derrida adds a further nuance to this position by distinguishing between two Heideggers: the logocentric, still humanist one who is philosophically responsible for the Nazi connection (so again the first of the four alternatives cited) but then also, on the perimeter of that figure, a second thinker—the once (pre-1933) and future (post-1935) Heidegger—who, even if for different reasons, escapes the terms of that characterization.

By this point in the discussion, the issues involved in the two matters of the relation between biography and philosophy, and the relation for Heidegger between his politics and his philosophy, have appeared in a number of formulations. Yet however one judges the conclusion drawn here in respect to those issues, an external question remains that encompasses them—inquiring about the reasons *behind* the large and continuing interest roused by the "Heidegger Question" itself. For there can be no doubt that this interest has been unusually intense and persistent, even allowing for the attention Heidegger would understandably claim as a central figure of twentieth-century philosophy. Is there a particular philosophical issue or a question in the sociology of knowledge behind this interest? Does its intensity reflect the *Schadenfreude* that might attend the fall of any important public figure, philosopher or not? Or again: would the allure be in the facts themselves—that is, in the drama of a connection between philosophy's abstract possibilities and the concrete determinacy of everyday life as these usually distant elements converge in Heidegger's Nazism?

There is no reason, of course, to force a choice among such alternatives, and probably elements of them all have been factors. It is clear, for example, that certain important philosophical issues are raised by Heidegger's coincident appearance in politics and in the history of philosophy. What is the systematic relation (if there is one) between political theory and metaphysics? More narrowly, does phenomenology or existentialism or "poststructuralism" as a theoretical "school" entail or even foster a common political or moral point of view? And more narrowly still (in a question I have tried to distinguish from these others), what connection is there between the biography of individual philosophers and the direction of their philosophical reflection? We might, for example, be bound to say of the philosopher, as Whitman did of the poet, "Who touches this book touches a man"—unless, that is, we turn to Gilbert Ryle's converse formulation quoted above and the claim that bad moral character would *ensure* "bad" philosophy. Even these provocations, however, do not seem to account for the unusual interest animating the many attempts to trace and to explain, moving variously to justify or to condemn, Heidegger's moral practice and his post-Holocaust silence. These attempts have been made recurrently in Germany itself but also and with as much force in France and more recently in the United States, often by critics who have otherwise hardly been concerned either with his philosophical writings more generally or with the Holocaust and Nazism in themselves.

Insofar as this side of Heidegger has drawn attention mainly within the academy, among philosophers and literary and social critics, one response to this question might go: "Of course; that is where Heidegger's prose of the world *would* matter. So many who have gathered round set out from the same concerns that he did; they would then, for some or all of his same reasons, have concurred in rejecting the 'humanistic' past, the foundationalist conceptions of knowledge and history, and the impersonalized present that ironically but consistently followed from it—seeking also a new beginning (once again) for thinking and, as it seemed, for being." Expressed here would be not only an affinity of spirit, but deference to an imagination that had demonstrated the possibility of that affinity.

And even where, by contrast, the interest in this Heidegger Question reflects antagonism, the same intensity of the provocation might be predicted for the response—with the temperature increasing on each side as the two react to each other. Thus, too, the hostility to Heidegger by political radicals and liberals, joining the more generally accepted criticism of his Nazi associations, would also lead readily to *Schadenfreude* as each new detail of his (on any account "nasty") history—whether deliberately concealed or not—emerged. And then in turn, the reaction against what his defenders saw as ad hominem irrelevancies (even when the assertions themselves were admitted as true) would be correspondingly, and increasingly, heated.

Even taking all this into account, however, neither singly nor together do the conceptual issues raised by his conduct or the consideration of professional affinity (and so also, defensiveness) or hostility seem by themselves adequate to account for the *fascination*—more than only the interest—sustained in Heidegger's history as that encompasses both his professional thought and his public conduct. Derrida, one of the few commentators who sees this phenomenon as an issue, explains the fascination as persisting "precisely because no one has ever been able to reduce Heidegger's thought in its entirety to that of a Nazi ideology"[5]—as if the interest was itself both a source for the attempts to accomplish that reduction and an expression of the frustration of failure. (Surely interest in Heidegger would fall dramatically, on Derrida's terms, for anyone claiming to have achieved the reduction Derrida refers to—and indeed many of Heidegger's critics at least believe they have succeeded in this, although without finding their interest diminished.)

With a question directed at so many different readers and kinds of readers, and with so many possible, and probable, causes, I venture still another account related to my thesis concerning the Jewish Question and the "Jewish Question"; namely, the connection disclosed in Heidegger between the life of the mind and its all-too-evident embodiment—not so much in philosophers' *persons* as in their public and common selves: a connection that in the academy has been constantly denied or, more exactly, repressed. It is as if the danger that Heidegger encountered and fell before evokes contrary but no less persistent and strong impulses, attracting at the same time as it repels: drawing spectators because the life of the mind rarely *matters* as it did in Heidegger's career; repelling them because of the course that that career took, whether accidentally or essentially, on Heidegger's own responsibility—though even then with a measure of attraction that wrongdoing itself may have (and not, of course, only for academics). Augustine in the *Confessions* recalls his pleasure as a young boy in stealing pears from a neighbor's trees—pleasure that he later recognized as coming from the act of stealing (and the company of his friends), not from the pears themselves which they then threw away. The reader's pleasure in Augustine's description is in turn related to the "confession" more than either to the stealing of the pears or to Augustine's own pleasure. His reading thus joins vicarious experience to a sense of immediacy: the combination of contingency and irrevocability—in short, of history—that accompanies any action, but especially wrongdoing, as much in the prospect as in the act itself, or perhaps more. There is, it seems to me, at least something of this "fatal attraction" in the allure of Heidegger's silence in the face of the Jewish Question.

For it is not only the combination of Heidegger's philosophical stature and his unhappy encounter with political power that has drawn attention to his conduct as a latter-day example of the *trahison des clercs*. Admittedly, Plato's two journeys to Syracuse are sometimes recalled as precedents (Hannah Arendt, in her tribute to Heidegger on his eightieth birthday, linked her exculpation of Heidegger's association with the Nazis to this analogy). But if Plato's trips ended in failure, no one accused him then or later of undertaking them in the face of, let alone in support of, moral enormity—nor was he open to criticism for having refused to acknowledge in its own terms what then became his failure. (The principal evidence we have about those journeys comes from a letter by Plato himself; we might here try to imagine the record we would have if we had to reconstruct Heidegger's history only from accounts that he provided.) It would obviously be circular to argue that the fascination with Heidegger's history is but another expression of the allure of evil and the impulse to disguise that response—and that we know this at least in part because of the fascination the Heidegger Question itself has aroused. But the hermeneutic circle of interpretation, as Heidegger himself represented it in the introduction to *Being and Time*, presumably applies also when it is Heidegger's own writing that is being interpreted;

whatever movement is possible in the circle, we may find here as well.

More directly and unavoidably than any other twentieth-century thinker, Heidegger has confronted the academy and its members with the question of the relation between thought and practice: practice not as armchair exercise or thought experiment, but as moral action. His most serious twentieth-century competitors for this title are Wittgenstein and Sartre. But the interest that attached itself to Wittgenstein (especially in England and the United States) was impelled less by the relation *in* him between philosophy and life than by his philosophical writings and his "practice" viewed separately, extreme and self-consuming as each of them was. And Sartre, who at one time was simply assumed to have outdone all other (including future) claims to the title, is now recalled more for what he wrote about the relation between thought and life than for his own embodiment of it—his practice but also his thinking having diminished in retrospect.[6] Viewed in terms of that relation, the academy's response to Heidegger's history expresses most immediately a desire for contact with the friction—the *non*fiction—of reality and life, of history that even through its silences does indeed address the questions it faces—combinations that otherwise often pass unrealized and untouched in the academy's insulated and abstract culture. And those who damn Heidegger, no less than those who praise him, might turn to him for this common reason before going on to turn against each other. Better even the "treason of the clerics" than the inanity of Philosophy 101.

HAVING COME THIS FAR in addressing Heidegger past and present, we reach a last question about the consequences of Heidegger's acts and words (or inaction and silence) for judging his own place in the history by which he judged others and would himself be judged; that is, in the history of philosophy. Does what has been said in these pages about Heidegger and the Jewish Question or the "Jewish Question" also bear on Heidegger's standing as a thinker—this writer and teacher often numbered among the most (on some accounts as *the* most) significant of twentieth-century philosophers? Even supposing for the moment that everything asserted here was indeed warranted, would that—*should* it—enter the assessment of Heidegger's philosophical importance? And if so, in what measure?

In this challenge the risk is evident of accepting the tempting but question-begging formula summarized by Lyotard in more general form than Ryle's earlier reference: "If a great thinker, then not a Nazi; if a Nazi, then not a great thinker."[7] That assertion might be defended in its general form or, more assuredly, as applicable to Heidegger in particular. But it cannot for either of these be arrived at apart from the claim that public practice and private (or professional) philosophy may or even must be internally related—the claim that has been made here specifically in respect to Heidegger's thought and practice.

This same contention, however, risks a conflict of interest in respect to the assessment of Heidegger as philosopher. To conclude that even if the claims made here were true they would make no difference to Heidegger's importance would place his answer of silence to the Jewish Questions in the realm of nonphilosophy—there adding one more historical and psychological narrative to the already large number that project a response to Jewish history based exclusively in feeling and seeing (or insensitivity and blindness), not, in any event, thinking. But the line of argument here has disputed this, insisting that Heidegger's silence on the Jewish Question and "Jewish Question" is not to be explained psychologically or personally—or parochially. Insisting still more emphatically that it is not the involuntary expression of taste or of a natural disposition. To the contrary: my claim has been that Heidegger's answer of silence is embedded in central themes and implications of his thinking: the status of Sein and Dasein, the nature and disclosure of Truth, the comportment of the individual in relation to the group. It would be prima facie implausible *not* to consider such a connection in assessing Heidegger the thinker—and insofar as the analysis here has found for the connection in Heidegger the thinker, it is just as implausible that the connection should have no consequences for his standing in that role.

Even readers sympathetic with my account up to this point might balk at this challenge. The "global" estimate of the importance of a philosopher, even if focused on the least time-bound elements of that achievement—thus the germ of the future—must be as much a gamble as it seems presumptuous. And we know historically that such assessments are intertwined with history itself; that even for the most important figures, assessments are unlikely to be concluded during a thinker's own lifetime or even within the bounds of a second generation as it struggles for its own space. Arguably there is *no* time when the question can be considered settled: philosophers seem in this respect closer to artists, who move in and out of the focus of public and professional interest, than to scientists, for whom the prospect of obsolescence is always a matter of when, not whether, it will take place.

Even the objections shaped in the preceding chapters to Heidegger's denial of the Jewish Question, and "Jewish Question," with the ground of that denial in the role he assigns to the concept of the Volk, may be contested on historical grounds drawn from philosophy itself. For however that criticism is judged, and even if it is linked centrally to his thinking, nothing there erases the undoubted attraction and influence Heidegger has had, an effect made evident in the testimony and to some extent the work of a number of other important Continental philosophers. These figures have themselves been forthright in acknowledging that effect, even when they have also announced their differences with him—specifically, insofar as they touch on it at all, with what has been represented here as his denial of the Jewish Question. Sartre, Merleau-Ponty, Lévinas, Arendt, Marcuse, Derrida, Gadamer: the common indebtedness is as clear and forceful as that recognized for any other twentieth-century philosopher by any group of influential "students" or successors. (The argument has been made that because none of these notable students associated themselves with him politically, it follows that Heidegger himself was not a Nazi[8]—although it is at least as plausible to conclude that these students found in him a teacher *notwithstanding* whatever in his thought conduced to Nazism.) The issue thus comes to this: How revealing of the *whole* is the philosophical failing alleged here in "Heidegger's silence"? And then, one step further: What implications does this have for what is otherwise celebrated in Heidegger's thought as its extraordinary—revolutionary—depth?

Even assuming a warrant for everything that has been proposed so far, I myself remain in doubt about these questions: skeptical of any assurance that the systematic grounds for what has emerged here as his denial of the Jewish Questions can (should) make no difference to Heidegger's "larger" standing, but wary of finding in those grounds the basis for a sweeping (and as the account here has viewed them, negative) judgment; yet also unwilling to accept categorically that it has *no* such general implication. This uncertainty might be seen as itself symptomatic, whether of the issue or the thinker. Indeed, one common distinction as it applies to Heidegger would underscore that tension here: the difference often asserted between thinkers who are important historically, for their influence on students and successors, and thinkers whose importance stems from their continuing power of philosophical illumination. As in the arts, so also in philosophy: preeminent figures like Plato, Aristotle, and Kant combine these qualities. Others fall into one or the other of the categories: thus the tradition, in the second, of "edifying" philosophers: Montaigne, Kierkegaard, Nietzsche. Heidegger has indisputably met the criterion of historical influence (given the relatively short time his students and successors have had). But the claims of his importance have often extended to the second criterion as well, of continuing or enlarging philosophical influence—and here the issue seems more in doubt. We are forced in any event to extrapolate from a narrow present, with only the shaky history of philosophical canonization in the past—of *other* philosophers—to serve as precedent.

And so, in effect, prediction becomes a matter of repetition forward—and so too the thesis that has been argued here as projected further: that as Heidegger's work (certainly the "later" Heidegger, but also the Heidegger of *Being and Time* and *The Basic Problems of Phenomenology*) meets philosophy's subsequent critical history, the issues around Heidegger's response to the "Jewish Question" and the Jewish Question will provide a continuing and severe test; that the metaphysical racism of which I have alleged that response is symptomatic—to which it has *attested*—will grow in importance rather than diminish, gaining authority as expressive of a whole: a specter that will not go away. At least some evidence for this projection is apparent in the extensive literature that sets out from Heidegger, and that concludes as either expository or, when it would build further on Heidegger, largely promissory. Where, philosophically, does Heidegger lead—other than to Heidegger himself? The most important of his students have not themselves become or remained "Heideggerians," nor have those students who remain Heideggerians found in him a means for critical development like that engendered by other figures in the history of philosophy. (It is not only Plato and Kant who through their substantial "neo-Platonic" or "neo-Kantian" traditions might serve as exemplars here, but also figures of a "second order" like Berkeley or Herder.)

The answer to the question of what philosophical steps come *after* Heidegger—in other words, what can be built on from him—has so far been equivocal. And though one could object against this assessment that too little time has passed to permit such judgment, or that "edifying" philosophy typically does *not* evoke systematic elaboration, the absence of speculative effect is at least suggestive. To be sure, individual parts of Heidegger's thought have been enlarged on in isolation from the others. So, for example, one current focus of interest in Heidegger has turned to his analysis of technology, at times taking that analysis as a basis for understanding the Holocaust itself—a formulation that seems as dramatically revisionist as any other in Holocaust historiography.[9] Still more emphatically, it might be held that the source of Heidegger's influence has been not in any particular doctrine, but in his challenge to philosophy as such, as the tradition that he criticized had defined its methods and goals and would, without him, have sustained its commitment to all of these. Indeed, this challenge, his heralding of "the *end* of philosophy" (as it had been), would account, as probably no other explanation does, for the responsiveness to Heidegger of the otherwise diverse group of important philosophers who then almost all set out in directions of their own. Yet if this challenge was an invitation to philosophical revolution, a question remains of how radical and sustained have been the changes that ensued, even in Heidegger himself but also and from the perspective of history, more importantly, in the others who responded to the invitation. There clearly *have been* revolutionary moments in the history of philosophy. But the *claim* of revolution is a standard trope of philosophical discourse, almost a commonplace, as what philosophy is remains philosophy's own first question. And the occurrence of revolution is not standard at all.

We do not require the Platonic view of a One overriding the Many, however, to recognize that although the central concepts of a philosophical project may later be appropriated singly, they often—depending on how central they had been in their first context—evoke also the other elements of that "whole." It is as viewed from this perspective that there obtrudes an issue superficially as circumscribed as Heidegger's answer of silence to the Jewish Question and then to the "Jewish Question"; one that will, I believe, continue in the afterlife of his work—post-Holocaust and post-post-Holocaust—because of its moral and metaphysical implications to affect estimates of his oeuvre. And to diminish it. Practical judgment exercised in or on history, we find here, applies also to even the deepest philosophical efforts or claims asserted in the name of thinking. Also in the lesson attested to by history's scrutiny of Heidegger, thinking presents itself as historically embodied, and here too we recognize the responsibility this imposes and the consequences of attempting to avoid it. On the one hand, thinking always sets itself in opposition to limits; on the other hand, thinkers—the vehicles of thinking—cannot escape *their* limits. One question that inevitably confronts all philosophers, then, is where they will set, or find, or submit to the limits of their thought and to what extent this determination may endanger what else they have said. More than any other twentieth-century philosopher, Heidegger attempted to break through the very notion of the limits of thinking, to override those boundaries at once in principle and in his own thought, to reach a point where the boundaries themselves would acknowledge and even welcome transgression. It is this aspiration that makes more notable an occasion on which Heidegger himself was willing to set, and to settle for, limits on his thought. There is a measure of irony and a measure also of justice in the fact that it was the Jewish Question and then later the "Jewish Question" that provided this occasion. And that the answer Heidegger proposed to them was silence.

A Conversation about Heidegger
with Eduard Baumgarten

DAVID LUBAN

[In a conversation with David Luban in spring 1993, I mentioned some of my thoughts about Heidegger's silence. In commenting on these David Luban recalled an encounter he had with Eduard Baumgarten, a figure who has emerged as of some importance in the discussion of Heidegger's history, and described a yet unpublished memoir that Luban had written about that meeting. He soon afterward sent me a copy of the memoir, which seemed to me a relevant addition to the complex pattern of Heidegger's biography and thinking—like all such reflections, open to interpretation, but certainly informative and in a number of respects quite pointed and not at all ambiguous. It occurred to me somewhat later that this book, with its discussion of Heidegger and the Jewish Question (and the "Jewish Question"), might provide a suitable context for publishing the memoir, and David Luban agreed (although, of course, without taking responsibility for any other part of the volume). The qualifications he notes about the credibility of certain parts of the memoir (in reference to Baumgarten's own ac-

David Luban is Morton and Sophia Macht Professor of Law at the University of Maryland at Baltimore and research scholar at the Institute for Philosophy and Public Policy, University of Maryland at College Park.

count) seem to me to anticipate questions that might be raised about it but even allowing for these, also to sustain the interest that the memoir itself has. —B. L.]

In 1976 I traveled in Germany with Michael Sukale, a philosopher who had studied with Eduard Baumgarten and had later edited *Gewissen und Macht,* a collection of Baumgarten's essays. We visited Baumgarten, then seventy-eight years old, at his home in Freiburg from 17 to 20 July 1976; during that visit we conversed at length about various philosophical topics. On 17 July we talked extensively about Baumgarten's relationship with Heidegger, which has emerged as an issue in recent debates about Heidegger's involvement with the Nazis. The following night I recorded the conversation in my diary, verifying some details with Baumgarten the next morning. A month later I wrote a detailed portrait of Baumgarten.

As it happens, Baumgarten painted a very distinctive portrait of Heidegger, one that may be of interest to readers who concern themselves with the question of Heidegger's Nazism as well as his attitude toward Jews. For that reason, I offer this narrative.

An important disclaimer: I am not myself a participant in the current debate about the extent of Heidegger's Nazi involvement. I vouch for the accuracy of my diary, but that is all. I made no independent attempt to verify anything Baumgarten told me, including dates or places. I cannot attest to the reliability of his memory, the extent to which his recollections were colored by his subsequent interpretation of Heidegger's motives, or even his veracity. On my assessment of what lawyers call his "demeanor evidence," however, I rate his honesty very high, especially since (as will be seen) he related several stories that paint an unflattering portrait of his own political courage. That he was willing to speak so openly about his own sins to an American Jew whom he knew to be preoccupied with the horrors of Nazism suggests a kind of honesty. My own view was that Baumgarten spoke in a confessional, not an apologetic, spirit; to shed some light on this, I include excerpts of a memoir of Baumgarten that I wrote a month after our meeting, as I was putting my diary in order. Perhaps

Baumgarten's charm and hospitality made me overly credulous; that is for readers to judge. I have included a few incidents from my diary not strictly connected with Heidegger in order to assist readers in forming an opinion about Baumgarten's reliability as well as my own.

One matter troubles me: I have a very clear recollection of Baumgarten relating one particular bit of information about Heidegger; but it is not in my diary. I shall nevertheless include it at the point in the narrative where my memory places it, flagging it there.

Memoir

As HE RELATED IT, Baumgarten's history with Heidegger is this. He met Heidegger in 1914.[1] Baumgarten told one interesting story from the early years with Heidegger. In 1922 Baumgarten became friends with Karl Mannheim, and Heidegger, on discovering this, remarked that Mannheim had stolen his ideas from Wilhelm Szilasi. Baumgarten confronted Mannheim with this, and Mannheim wrote an angry letter to Heidegger. Baumgarten also wrote to Heidegger, saying he had told Mannheim about Heidegger's accusation. He added that since Heidegger was the older man, he must eat (*fressen*) this—that is, swallow what Baumgarten had done. Heidegger wrote back a letter beginning "Er hats gefressen" and going on to say that philosophy must be done with passion, even when passion runs very high.

After obtaining his Ph.D. Baumgarten traveled to America, where from 1924 to 1929 he studied, worked at odd jobs (he mentioned two, as a waiter in Chicago and a gardener in New Hampshire), and taught at the University of Wisconsin. His wife taught there as well, as M. I. Rostovzeff's assistant in the history department. Baumgarten recalled that she astounded people by learning two hundred students' names in a week. This was a rather sad reminiscence because in 1976, although she remained physically vigorous, she was unable to remember a conversation from one minute to the next. In 1929 he returned to Germany to study with

Heidegger, and he was Heidegger's assistant until 1931. Baumgarten recalled sitting with Husserl and Heidegger as Husserl made a sentimental speech on the theme "we are three generations of phenomenologists." Heidegger broke with Baumgarten during a dramatic meeting of Heidegger's seminar in 1932, and Baumgarten habilitated with Jaspers, then taught at Göttingen, a position he obtained partly through the good offices of Husserl. His writings concerned American philosophy: he wrote a book on Benjamin Franklin and another on pragmatism.

In 1935 his university career was threatened because of a letter of denunciation written by Heidegger. After the war Baumgarten advocated Heidegger's denazification, and Heidegger subsequently wrote him two reconciliatory letters.

Baumgarten attributed his difficulties with Heidegger to personal animus rather than political conviction. In his view, three incidents turned Heidegger against him.

First: When Heidegger moved to Freiburg his wife fell in love, by coincidence, with the very house Baumgarten lived in. She ordered the architect of her own house to copy the outer proportions, which he did. Baumgarten was studying on a fellowship. During their American stay Baumgarten's wife had earned $3,500, which they assumed was lost in the 1929 crash. It was not, and a couple of years later she was sent a check for the full amount. In Germany this was an extraordinary sum of money, and the Baumgartens bought the house in question. They showed its picture to Heidegger. Shortly afterward the dean, Wilhelm von Möllendorf, told Baumgarten that if he was thinking of habilitating under Heidegger, he should forget it. Heidegger had charged that Baumgarten was a fraud, accepting a stipend when he was loaded with money; Baumgarten, in Heidegger's view, had evidently been corrupted by America.

Möllendorf arranged a meeting between the Baumgartens and the Heideggers to clear the air. The story was straightened out, and Möllendorf pointed out that it was entirely proper for a wife to get money for her family while the husband attended the university on a stipend. Heidegger, still miffed, replied that perhaps this was American thinking, but in Germany one still distinguished between putting aside money for one's family and purchasing a *Schloss*. (Möllendorf remarked to Baumgarten as they left, "Heidegger may be a great man, but at heart he is still a petit bourgeois.")

Second: Heidegger delivered the lecture "What Is Metaphysics?" in Heidelberg, receiving extravagant compliments thereafter from Max Weber's brother, Alfred, and the literary critic Friedrich Gundolf. (Weber simply clasped his hands and said, *Wunderbar!* while Gundolf toasted Heidegger, saying the lecture had taught him that poetry has the next-to-last word, but philosophy has the last.) When Heidegger reported his triumph to Baumgarten, the latter said that he was sure Gundolf, at least, had not been sincere ("He is from Darmstadt, so he is polite"), since otherwise he would have been insulting Stefan George.[2] Heidegger's vanity evidently was wounded, for he sent Baumgarten to Heidelberg to spy out the real situation. Baumgarten spoke with Marianne Weber (Baumgarten's aunt: he was Max Weber's nephew and literary executor). She told him that, whereas Jaspers had commented that "in language alone it is sheer musicality," during Heidegger's lecture Gundolf had whispered a sarcastic comment to her.

On his return, Baumgarten baited Heidegger a bit by gossiping about unrelated matters; when Heidegger impatiently demanded his report, Baumgarten replied that his trip had corroborated Heidegger's theory that the essence of truth is ambiguity. Heidegger: "What do you mean?" Baumgarten: "Gundolf praised you to your face but joked about you to others. That is ambiguous, so it must be true." Heidegger got up from his desk and stood in the corner of the room whistling, a sign that he was barely under control. Baumgarten believed that Heidegger did not forgive him for this episode.

Third: One day Baumgarten and Heidegger rode the tram to the university together. As they got off, a young man approached Heidegger, his face full of enthusiasm, hero-worshiping. Baumgarten tactfully withdrew and afterward asked Heidegger who this man was. Heidegger replied: "Oh, some Jew." Baumgarten says that this remark wrenched his insides. Heidegger, as always, stopped to buy a long, thin cigar, but talking with the young man on the tram made him late to his lecture. Consequently, when Heidegger and Baumgarten entered the room it was quiet, and Baumgarten overheard a conversation. A Japanese student in the first row asked the man next to him, "How long have you studied with Heidegger?" The man whispered, "Fifteen years," and the Japanese replied, "Oh, I see—yes, you even look like Heidegger." As it happened, the man was Jewish, and very Jewish in appearance.

When Baumgarten and Heidegger went home that night, Heidegger remarked that he had guests from Japan. Baumgarten asked whether the man at the lecture was among them, and Heidegger said, "Yes, and he's the best—an excellent interpreter of texts." Baumgarten asked innocently: "Don't you think that a good interpreter of texts is also a good interpreter of physiognomies?" Heidegger said yes, and Baumgarten repeated the conversation from the lecture hall. Heidegger was furious, and Baumgarten remarked that this incident probably sealed his fate with Heidegger.

Baumgarten's break with Heidegger occurred on 13 January (?—I cannot quite read my own handwriting here) 1932, which Baumgarten referred to as "Hilarious Day." Baumgarten had to present an exposition of a chapter in Kant at Heidegger's seminar. He wrote on the categorical imperative, maintaining that whereas Heidegger emphasized Kant's ambiguities, Kant here was unequivocal in identifying the essence of humanity with the possibility of distinguishing among motives. For some reason Heidegger became furious. He turned to Helene Weiss, another student (whom, Baumgarten remarked, the seminar members all referred to as the *jüdische Gretchen*), and said: "There were five points to be discussed; did Baumgarten's thesis do this?" She turned pale and did not answer, so Heidegger turned to the student next to her (a veteran of his seminar), who dutifully replied, "No, Herr Professor." Heidegger remarked that Baumgarten was not competent to expound a chapter of Kant, then put his fist on the table and said witheringly, "According to you, one must be a good human being before beginning to philosophize." Baumgarten placed his own fist on the table and said, "I protest this interpretation of my work."

Baumgarten knew he was now finished with Heidegger. He went to Husserl and told him this. To his astonishment, Husserl rang for wine and toasted Baumgarten's liberation. When Baumgarten related the full story of the seminar, Husserl said, "What? You *protested* his interpretation of your work? You should have said, 'Herr Professor, you understand my point exactly—and it is Kant's point too.'" Later Husserl helped Baumgarten write letters to Heidegger. (Baumgarten: "Husserl, who could talk for three hours about phenomenology in such a way that you couldn't understand a word of it, kept telling me that I wasn't saying plainly what I meant.")

For a week after Hilarious Day, students in the seminar protested to Heidegger about his treatment of Baumgarten. Among them was Herbert Marcuse (Baumgarten: "That fellow on the left in California, what's his name?"), who remarked to Baumgarten that his error had been to say something novel in a seminar. Soon after, Heidegger wrote to the Lincoln Foundation, which was paying Baumgarten's fellowship, and told the officers that Baumgarten was incompetent, thereby costing him the fellowship.

Husserl helped Baumgarten obtain a position in Göttingen. In 1935 Baumgarten was told that he was fired, that he should go back to America, and that he must ask no questions. A friend of Frau Baumgarten, however, was a secretary in the office of the Nazi functionary in the university. She told Baumgarten that if he came the next day, while her boss was in Hildesheim, she would show him his dossier. He discovered in it the now well-known letter of denunciation from Heidegger, stating that Baumgarten was incompetent and faulty in character, that he was part of the liberal-democratic circle of Max Weber in Heidelberg, that he might have an understanding of America but was deficient in political instinct, that Heidegger supposed Baumgarten's friendship with the Jew Fränkel had gotten him his position in Göttingen and explained his present social circles, that in Freiburg Baumgarten was anything but a National Socialist, that it was just as impossible to take him into the SA [Sturmabteilung—the Nazi Party's private army] as into the ranks of the university, and so on.

Baumgarten copied this letter by hand in the functionary's office, and it was this copy that I saw. (In 1976 I did not read German, and Baumgarten and Sukale translated the letter for me.) Baumgarten explained to me that Heidegger's remark about his present social circles was a reference to the fact that Baumgarten played in a string quartet with three Jews. If accurate, this explanation seems to be a disturbing indicator of antisemitism on Heidegger's part. However, I do not find the comment recorded in my diary. I am nevertheless certain that Baumgarten made it.

According to Baumgarten, Heidegger had written the letter two years before, but the Nazi functionary's predecessor had dismissed it as mere spleen. Baumgarten also explained that Heidegger's remark about the Jew Fränkel proved to be his salvation. Baumgarten did not know Fränkel, and it was the Jew Husserl who had gotten him his job; but (according to Baumgarten) Heidegger was not yet in a position where he could have gotten away with impugning Husserl. Hence he named Fränkel instead. Baumgarten approached the Nazi functionary and said that it had come to his attention that he was fired because of his association with Fränkel. Baumgarten then took an oath that he did not know Fränkel and thereby discredited Heidegger's letter and saved his job.

In 1937 Baumgarten, the erstwhile admirer of Benjamin Franklin and American pragmatism, joined the Nazi Party. After the war Baumgarten was labeled a "top Nazi" by the British because—he claimed—the BBC had mistranslated a radio speech he had made. Baumgarten fled to the French zone, where he showed the texts of the two versions of his speech to the French general Pierre Koenig. As a consequence he was denazified, though he admitted candidly that this was in large part because his father had been a teacher of Koenig's adjutant.

These circumstances may have led to his final exchange with Heidegger. As Baumgarten explains it, Jaspers was asked by the Allies whether Heidegger should be rehabilitated. Jaspers sent a "balanced" reply, including a copy of Heidegger's letter of denunciation against Baumgarten (which he had obtained from Marianne Weber) as well as a letter Heidegger had written to help Werner Brock, a Jew, escape to England. Nevertheless, the letter about Baumgarten made the more powerful impression, and it damned Heidegger.

Baumgarten wrote angrily to Jaspers, saying that Jaspers had no right to use his letter without permission; at that time, he said, the enemy had been within Germany, but now it came from *Ausland*, whereas Heidegger was a countryman who in these circumstances should be defended. Heidegger heard about this and sent Baumgarten a reconciliatory letter. Heidegger wanted a meeting with Baumgarten; Baumgarten believes that Heidegger wanted him to use his influence with the French general on his behalf. This meeting, however, Baumgarten did not consent to. In a second letter Heidegger told Baumgarten that he was now moving in distant reaches of thought, and he wished Baumgarten good luck on the outside. Baumgarten believed this meant "outside the university" and found it ironic that he was permitted to resume teaching whereas Heidegger was not.

Heidegger's letter of denunciation reveals prima facie a man of substantial Nazi conviction. Baumgarten's portrait of Heidegger is different: it shows a man who was driven not so much by political or ideological passions as by personal pettiness, more than usual vanity, and a desire for philosophical glory. (Baumgarten recollected that at one point Heidegger was working through a pile of Marxist writings so that he would be in a position to reign as *der deutsche Philosoph* no matter who prevailed in the ensuing political struggle.) His portrait also reveals a man possessing a measure of—at least—social antisemitism.

And what of Baumgarten? In my diary I find myself remarking on his "openness, his lack of pretension, his nonchalance." Baumgarten told me quite freely about his denazification; Sukale remarked to me later that in Germany *nobody* who had been labeled a "top Nazi" ever talked about it to anyone, let alone to an American Jew. I asked Baumgarten directly what he knew of the "Final Solution" at the time. He answered that he knew nothing about it, but then he admitted that if he had had the desire to know he could have found out. To illustrate what he meant, he told me a story about a young man he knew, a soldier back on leave from the East, and his sister. The soldier burst into tears in the sister's presence—and she would not ask him why. Baumgarten implied that he was like the sister.

He seemed to have an abiding affection for America and Americana. His decor included an "aerial" map of New York City dated 1907, and his workroom had a sign in English: I Can't Solve Your Problems, but I Can Help You Enjoy Them. One of Baumgarten's favorite bits of Americana was a sign he had seen on a New York store: Visit Us While We Move. To Baumgarten this slogan epitomized America, and he repeated it again and again during our visit. When I left he presented me with a booklet he had written on Benjamin Franklin, titled *On the Art of Compromise* (*Von der Kunst des Kompromisses*).

In addition to our conversations about Heidegger, other incidents in the visit made a strong impression on me. The third evening, Baumgarten brought out and carefully unwrapped Max Weber's death mask, which (I wrote) had an "uncanny ghostly feeling." Less weird, but equally striking, was Baumgarten's pencil sketch of Husserl that hung on the wall. Baumgarten was a talented violinist who had studied with Adolph Busch. Though he complained that his playing had deteriorated during the past year (and his tone was indeed a bit shaky), he and his wife gave a fine performance of a Schubert sonatina (op. 137), and Baumgarten played the Bach Chaconne beautifully.

I quote from my diary, 18 August 1976:

"Baumgarten approaches: a vigorous, slightly stooped man with glad, twinkling eyes behind spectacles, hair which falls onto his forehead, mouth permanently puckish and looking as though laughter is always at his lips. (In this I am not disappointed: I have never met a man of such excellent humor. Early the first evening, Sukale calls Baumgarten a 'Master of Insults,' and for the next four days Baumgarten periodically recalls it—'Master of Insults!'—and bursts into laughter.) . . .

"In 1937, the author of the book on American democracy had joined the Nazi Party. This is the real paradox of Baumgarten, one that he has been trying to explain to himself ever since. Since the end of the war . . . his main project, his all-consuming passion, . . . has been a study of Hitler. . . . He delves deeper and deeper, in an effort to understand not just Hitler, but himself. . . . He talks of how during the war his main feeling was one of elation. Now he labors on in a monumental effort of honesty, an accountant trying to balance the books of his own life.

"And within a few short weeks before we arrived, Baumgarten wrote his book. But it is not a study of Hitler: it is his own memoirs, written in three thick volumes. And—such is the honesty of this man—he has left every second page blank so that others can go through and correct his memory where he has whitewashed or varnished over the truth. The book is called *Spielraum unter Hitler.* [*Spielraum* is a technical word meaning 'tolerance' in the sense used in the milling of precision machine parts.] His theme, in other words, is a discussion not of Hitler's totalitarianism, but rather a firsthand account of the opposite, of the *Spielraum* in the Third Reich. . . .

"Baumgarten says: 'My book will be the first about a middle-level man working his way through hell—only it didn't seem so hellish—in fact, he rather enjoyed it.'"

NOTES

1. Bruno Bauer, *Die Juden-Frage,* in *Deutschen Jahrbücher für Wissenschaft und Kunst* 5 (1842); Karl Marx, *Zur Judenfrage* (1844), trans. in *Marx: Early Writings,* ed. T. B. Bottomore (New York: McGraw-Hill, 1964); Hermann Cohen, *Ein Bekenntnis in der Judenfrage* (Berlin: F. Dummler, 1880); Theodor Herzl, *Der Judenstaat: Versuch einer modernen Lösung der Judenfrage* (Vienna: M. Breitenstein, 1896); Jean-Paul Sartre, *Réflexions sur la Question Juive* (Paris: P. Morihen, 1946); Ahad Ha'am, "Siman Ha-Sh'aylah," in *Collected Essays* (Berlin: Jüdischer Verlag, 1921); L. N. Tolstoy, *Ueber Antisemitism un die Yiddishen Frage* (New York: S. Druckerman, 1910); V. I. Lenin, *Natzionale un Yiddishe-Frage* (Moscow: Central Publications of USSR, 1927); Louis D. Brandeis, *The Jewish Problem: How to Solve It* (New York: Zionist Organization of America, 1939); Henry Ford, *The Jewish Question* (London: MCP, 1938). The earliest citation of "die jüdische Frage" is referred to 1838 (Rena R. Auerbach, ed., *The "Jewish Question" in German-Speaking Countries, 1848–1914: A Bibliography* [New York: Garland, 1994], p. xi). On the history of the phrase the "Jewish Question," see Alex Bein, *The Jewish Question,* trans. Harry Zohn (New York: Herzl Press, 1990).

2. For reasons discussed in Berel Lang, *Act and Idea in the Nazi Genocide* (Chicago: University of Chicago Press, 1990), I attempt to avoid the term "the Holocaust" in my own writing because of what seems to me the misrepresentation echoed from its biblical origins and its reference to a form of sacrifice. This dissent from the English-language convention (the Hebrew, Yiddish, and French seem to me preferable) is an uphill and perhaps losing struggle—but use of the term in this book is not so much an admis-

sion of defeat as a citation of its use by other writers, since the focus of discussion here starts with the way others represent that event (and thus by implied or—sometimes—explicit quotation marks).

3. On the "affiliative" relation between the Enlightenment and the Holocaust, see Berel Lang, "Genocide and Kant's Enlightenment," in *Act and Idea in the Nazi Genocide*.

4. As Jürgen Habermas has pointed out, what is at issue here is not the relation between the *life* and the work of Heidegger, since that formulation begs the crucial question whether Heidegger's political views should be considered part of his work. See *The New Conservatism*, trans. S. W. Nicolsen (Cambridge: MIT Press, 1992), chap. 6.

5. The topics thus introduced seem to have established a rhetoric of quotation marks: so, for example, Jean-François Lyotard's *Heidegger and "the jews"* [in contrast to—the Jews], trans. Andreas Michel and Mark S. Roberts (Minneapolis: University of Minnesota Press, 1990), and Jacques Derrida's *Of Spirit: Heidegger and the Question*, trans. Geoffrey Bennington and Rachel Bowlby (Chicago: University of Chicago Press, 1989), which focuses on the difference between Heidegger's references to '*Geist*' and to "*Geist*." To be sure, the positions asserted in these (and my) accounts differ—including the substantive question of where the quotation marks should be applied.

6. At least as concerns its literal appearance, there has been little disagreement about the *fact* of Heidegger's silence. (see, e.g., Derrida, *Of Spirit*; Victor Farias, *Heidegger and Nazism* (Philadelphia: Temple University Press, 1989); Luc Ferry and Alain Renaut, *Heidegger et les modernes* (Paris: Grasset, 1988); "Symposium on Heidegger and Nazism," ed. Arnold Davidson, *Critical Inquiry* 15 (1989): 407–88; Gunther Neske and Emil Kettering, *Martin Heidegger and National Socialism*, trans. Lisa Harries (New York: Paragon House, 1990). What divides the accounts of Heidegger's silence is the issue of how to understand or to explain it.

7. Jacques Derrida poses the first of these formulations ("Heidegger's Silence," in Neske and Kettering, *Martin Heidegger and National Socialism*); Heidegger himself is probably the initiator and in any event remains the most persistent advocate of the second formulation, beginning with his "denazification" hearings soon after the end of the war.

8. A vivid formulation of this view appears in Shoshana Felman and Dori Laub, *Testimony: Crises of Witnessing in Literature, Psychoanalysis, and History* (New York: Routledge, 1992)—not quite vivid enough, however, to overcome the view's nonfalsifiability.

9. For the purposes of this book, I have taken 1945 as the dividing line between the pre- and post-Holocaust periods. The genocide of the Jews had begun four years before that, in the summer of 1941; but 1945 marks the point at which the genocide stopped after Germany's formal surrender

and, more important, the point at which there can be no doubt of Heidegger's being aware of its occurrence.

NOTES TO CHAPTER TWO

1. Cited in Hugo Ott, *Martin Heidegger: A Political Life*, trans. Allan Blunden (New York: Basic Books, 1993), p. 348.

2. Hannah Arendt, "For Martin Heidegger's Eightieth Birthday," reprinted in Neske and Kettering, *Martin Heidegger and National Socialism*, p. 210.

3. See Robert Faurisson, *Memoir en défense* (Paris: La Vieille Taupe, 1980); Paul Rassinier, *Drame des Juifs européens* (Paris: Sept Couleurs, 1964); Arthur Butz, *The Hoax of the Twentieth Century* (Torrance, Calif.: Noontide Press, 1977).

4. I introduce this distinction for the sake of argument and because it would be easier (if the evidence required this) to override it later than to introduce it retroactively. Clearly, the distinction poses a substantive question: What *is* the relation between Heidegger's "public" or exoteric statements and his more deliberately and technically philosophical texts? That the two were typically directed to different audiences is no doubt true— but neither this nor other stylistic differences by themselves *entail* a substantive discontinuity between the two forms (a position asserted by Richard Rorty; see below, chapter 4). I propose elsewhere (Berel Lang, *The Anatomy of Philosophical Style* [Oxford: Basil Blackwell, 1990]) that stylistic evidence in this and other philosophical writing argues for continuity between those two domains of writing. To avoid this issue here, however, I treat the two categories separately—although the distinction turns out to be difficult to sustain even when one tries to do so.

5. Cited by Wolfgang Schirmacher, *Technik und Gelassenheit* (Freiburg: Alber, 1983), p. 25. See also the discussion of the Bremen lectures in Rudiger Safranski, *Ein Meister aus Deutschland: Heidegger und seine Zeit* (Munich: Hanser, 1994), pp. 450–51, and Johannes Fritsche, "On Brinks and Bridges in Heidegger," *Graduate Faculty Philosophy Journal* 18 (1995): 161–62, 167–73.

6. "Agriculture is now the mechanized food industry. Air is now set upon to yield nitrogen, the earth to yield ore, ore to yield uranium, for example; uranium is set upon to yield atomic energy, which can be released either for destruction or for peaceful use" ("The Question concerning Technology," in Martin Heidegger, *The Question concerning Technology and Other Essays*, trans. William Lovitt [New York: Harper and Row, 1977]). The original statement appears in "Das Ge-Stell," from "Bremen Vorträge 1949," in *Gesamtausgabe*, vol. 79 (Frankfurt am Main: Klostermann, 1994), p. 27.

7. Ibid., p. 56.

8. I am indebted to David Luban for calling attention to this anticipation.

9. Cf. Ernst Nolte, *Das Vergehen der Vergangenheit: Antwort an meine Kritiker in sogenannten Historikerstreit* (Berlin: Ullstein, 1987).

10. If it was not—and the balance of evidence points in that direction (see Rainer Martin, "Ein rassistisches Konzept von Humanität," *Badische Zeitung*, 19–20 December 1987)—then Heidegger's claim to the contrary (e.g., in the *Spiegel* interview) is at least mistaken and possibly a lie. For purposes of this discussion, however, the parenthetical expression is no less suggestive about Heidegger's silence than the assertion of National Socialism's "inner truth and greatness" would be by itself.

11. Martin Heidegger, *What Is Called Thinking?* trans. J. Glenn Gray (New York: Harper and Row, 1968), p. 66. This book derives from the first series of lectures (1951–52) Heidegger gave at the University of Freiburg after his postwar reinstatement to the faculty as professor emeritus.

12. Reprinted in Richard Wolin, ed., *The Heidegger Controversy: A Critical Reader* (Cambridge: MIT Press, 1993), p. 161.

13. Heidegger did give a television interview after the *Spiegel* interview took place, on the occasion of his eightieth birthday (broadcast on 24 September 1969). In the preparatory discussion for that later interview, however, he made it clear to Richard Wisser, the interviewer, that he would not address questions concerning his own political past or, by implication, about the Nazi period more generally. (He mentioned to Wisser that these had been taken up in the *Spiegel* interview.) See Richard Wisser, "Afterthoughts and Gratitude," in Neske and Kettering, *Martin Heidegger and National Socialism*, pp. 89–124.

14. See Ott, *Martin Heidegger*, pp. 188–89.

15. The "Law for the Restoration of the Professional Civil Service," which called for the exclusion of Jewish faculty, had been issued before Heidegger took office; thus he knew, in assuming the rectorship, the details of the policy he would be obliged to implement. The task was easier, moreover, because a number of Jewish faculty members were already being forced out of the university when he took office; indeed, they were denied the right to vote in the "near-unanimous" Senate election that brought Heidegger the rectorship (cf. Hugo Ott, *Unterwegs zu seiner Biographie* [Frankfurt: Campus, 1988], p. 171).

16. This statement conflicts with an earlier one—in his 1945 letter to the chairman of the university denazification commission—in which he says he did *not* write to Frau Husserl because of "the bitter sense of shame I now felt about what was being done to the Jews" (Ott, *Unterwegs*, p. 173).

17. The statement appeared in the *Freiburger Studentenzeitung*, 3 November 1933. It is almost certainly about these lines that Heidegger writes, in his letter to Marcuse: "A few sentences in [the statement] I regard today

as a slip [*Entgleisung*]. That is all." It seems fair to ask whether any pair of statements by a serious philosopher—off duty or on duty—approach the usurpation of metaphysics by ideology evident here.

18. Farias gives a conflicting account of that meeting. See Farias, *Heidegger and Nazism*, p. 131.

19. Cited in Wolin, *Heidegger Controversy*, pp. 62, 64.

20. Rockmore makes the point that since the unpublished Heidegger papers have been largely under the editorial control of his family or his advocates, it is more likely that on contentious issues, material favorable to him would have already been released—with the material still unreleased, if it bears on such matters at all, weighing on the other side (Tom Rockmore, *On Heidegger's Nazism and Philosophy* [Berkeley: University of California Press, 1992], p. 299). Elzbieta Ettinger had access to some of the hitherto restricted Heidegger-Arendt correspondence (*Hannah Arendt / Martin Heidegger* [New Haven: Yale University Press, 1995]); but her work does not suggest any substantial revisions in Heidegger's views. (See Berel Lang, "Snowblind: Martin Heidegger and Hannah Arendt," *The New Criterion* 14 [1996]: 5–9.)

21. Letter to rector of University of Freiburg, 4 November 1945; cited in Wolin, *Heidegger Controversy*, p. 64.

22. In Leo Strauss, *Persecution and the Art of Writing* (Glencoe, Ill.: Free Press, 1952). To be sure, Heidegger himself does not make this association.

23. For a critical discussion of this—limitless—defense of Heidegger's silence, see Rockmore, *On Heidegger's Nazism*, p. 202. Although, like his advocates, Heidegger provides no criterion for distinguishing which silences should count as "speaking," he himself laid the ground for this position in such statements as "Man speaks by being silent" (Heidegger, *What Is Called Thinking?* p. 16).

24. Derrida, *Of Spirit*, p. 147

NOTES TO CHAPTER THREE

1. For an incisive summary of both the process and the issues involved, see Jacob Katz, *Exclusiveness and Tolerance* (Oxford: Oxford University Press, 1961).

2. So, for example, in Lessing's *Nathan der Weise* (1779) and the less-known *Die Erziehung des Menschengeschlechts* (1780); Herder's *Ideen zur Philosophie der Geschichte der Menschheit* (1784–91); Fichte's *Beitrag zur Berichtung der Urteile des Publikums über die Französische Revolution — zur Beurteilung ihrer Rechtmässigkeit* (published anonymously, 1793).

3. Marlene Zarader, in *La dette impensée: Heidegger et l'héritage hébraïque* (Paris: Editions du Seuil, 1990), attempts to show an indebtedness on Hei-

degger's part to the "Hebrew" tradition (see esp. pp. 180–83)—with results that at best seem strained and, even if accepted, invoke his work so obliquely that they do not alter my contention here.

4. This interpretation was suggested by Baumgarten himself, as reported in the memoir by David Luban—"A Conversation about Heidegger with Eduard Baumgarten"—which appears as an appendix to this book.

5. Farias, *Heidegger and Nazism*, p. 161.

6. For a conspectus of these "philosophical radicals," see Hans Sluga, *Heidegger's Crisis: Philosophy and Politics in Nazi Germany* (Cambridge: Harvard University Press, 1993), chap. 6.

7. Neske and Kettering, *Martin Heidegger and National Socialism*, p. 158.

8. Karl Jaspers, "Philosophical Autobiography," in *The Philosophy of Karl Jaspers*, ed. P. A. Schilp, 2d ed. (LaSalle, Ill.: Open Court, 1981), p. 75.

9. Derrida, *Of Spirit*, p. 74.

10. Made 11 November 1933; cited in Guido Schneeberger, *Nachlese zu Heidegger* (Bern: Suhr, 1962), p. 149.

11. *Freiburger Studentenzeitung*, January 1934; cited in Schneeburger, *Nachlese zu Heidegger*, p. 181.

12. Martin Heidegger, *Heraklit*, in *Gesamtausgabe*, vol. 55 (Frankfurt am Main: Klostermann, 1979), p. 123.

13. Martin Heidegger, *Introduction to Metaphysics*, trans. Ralph Manheim (New Haven: Yale University Press, 1959), p. 50.

14. Martin Heidegger, *Einführung in die Metaphysik*, in *Gesamtausgabe*, vol. 40 (Frankfurt am Main: Klostermann, 1983), pp. 41–42.

15. Martin Heidegger, *Parmenides*, in *Gesamtausgabe*, vol. 54 (Frankfurt am Main: Klostermann, 1982), p. 144.

16. Martin Heidegger, *Beiträge zur Philosophie*, in *Gesamtausgabe*, vol. 65 (Frankfurt am Main: Klostermann, 1989), p. 42.

17. Martin Heidegger, *Hölderlin's Hymnen "Germanien" und "Der Rhein,"* in *Gesamtausgabe*, vol. 39 (Frankfurt am Main: Klostermann, 1980), p. 121.

18. Martin Heidegger, "The Self-Assertion of the German University," trans. Karsten Harries, *Review of Metaphysics* 38 (1985): 474–75.

19. Martin Heidegger, *Letter on Humanism*, trans. Frank A. Capuzzi, in *Martin Heidegger: Basic Writings*, ed. David Krell (New York: Harper and Row, 1977), p. 217.

20. From a speech by Heidegger, 22 January 1934. See Wolin, *Heidegger Controversy*, p. 56.

21. Heidegger, *Beiträge zur Philosophie*, p. 117.

22. Heidegger, *Grundfragen der Philosophie*, in *Gesamtausgabe*, vol. 45 (Frankfurt am Main: Klostermann, 1984), p. 2.

23. Interview with Heidegger, "Nur noch ein Gott kann uns retten," *Der Spiegel*, 31 May 1976, p. 217.

24. Heidegger, *Introduction to Metaphysics*, p. 57.

25. Derrida, *Of Spirit*, p. 68. For a systematic critique of Heidegger's "mythologizing" of Greek, see John Caputo, "Why Aletheia Is Not a Greek Word," in *Demythologizing Heidegger* (Bloomington: Indiana University Press, 1993), pp. 21–29.

26. Robert Bernasconi, "'I Will Tell You Who You Are': Heidegger on Greco-German Destiny and *Amerikanismus*," in *From Phenomenology to Thought, Errancy, and Desire*, ed. Babette Babich (Dordrecht: Kluwer, 1995).

27. Heidegger, *Introduction to Metaphysics*, pp. 102–3; Martin Heidegger, *Being and Time*, trans. John Macquarrie and Edward Robinson (New York: Harper and Row, 1962), p. 80; Heidegger, *What Is Called Thinking?* pp. 139–47.

28. Draft of letter to Johann Heinrich Voss (May 1805), cited in Walter Kaufmann, Introduction to Friedrich Nietzsche, *The Genealogy of Morals* (New York: Vintage, 1969), p. 6.

29. Cf. A. N. Whitehead, *Science and the Modern World* (New York: Macmillan, 1925), chap. 3.

30. See on this dispute Bernd Martin, "Einführung," in *Martin Heidegger und das "Dritte Reich"* (Darmstadt: Wissenschaftliche Buchgesellschaft, 1989); see also "A 1951 Dialogue on Interpretation: Emil Staiger, Martin Heidegger, and Leo Spitzer," trans. B. Lang and C. Ebel, *PMLA* 105 (1990): 409–35.

31. Sluga, *Heidegger's Crisis*, p. 175. One could, I suppose, mention here the claim by Hitler himself at the opening of the Great German Art Exhibition (18 July 1937) that "never was mankind closer to antiquity in its external appearance and feeling than it is today" (cited in the New York Public Library catalog of the exhibition, "Assault on the Arts").

32. Martin Heidegger, *Der Feldweg* (Frankfurt am Main: Klostermann, 1956), p. 4.

33. Heidegger, *What Is Called Thinking?* p. 17.

34. Martin Heidegger, "On the Essence of Truth," in *Heidegger: Basic Writings*, ed. David Krell (New York: Harper and Row, 1977), pp. 128–29.

35. For a collection of comments that at once attest to and exaggerate such common elements (by, e.g., Beaufret, LeFebvre, Chatelet, Axelos), see Pierre Bourdieu, *The Political Ontology of Martin Heidegger*, trans. Peter Collier (Stanford: Stanford University Press, 1991), pp. 94–95.

36. Martin Heidegger, "The Self–Assertion of the University," trans. William S. Lewis, in Wolin, *Heidegger Controversy*, p. 34. Defending his criticism in the Rectoral Address of the traditional academic freedom, in the *Spiegel* interview (1966) Heidegger would say, "I still stand by it."

37. Maurice Blanchot, "Thinking the Apocalypse," trans. Paula Wissing, *Critical Inquiry* 15 (1989): 479.

38. A basis for this claim appears in *Being and Time* (1927) as well as in the writings after that, although the reliance on a mediating historical or social form is sufficiently muted in the former to permit a commentator

like Dreyfus to identify *self*-interpretation as determinative (cf. Hubert Dreyfus, *Being-in-the-World: A Commentary on Heidegger's "Being and Time"* [Cambridge: MIT Press, 1991], p. 23). This does not, however, contravert the importance Heidegger attaches to what I have referred to as mediation; so, for example, his claim that since "fateful Dasein, as Being-in-the-world, exists essentially in Being-with-others, its historicizing is a cohistoricizing and is determinative for it as *destiny*. This is how we designate the historicizing of the community, of a people. Destiny is not something that puts itself together out of individual fates, any more than Being-with-one-another can be conceived as the occurring together of several subjects" (*Being and Time*, p. 436).

39. Cited in Ott, *Martin Heidegger*, p. 229.

40. Martin Heidegger, *Nietzsche*, trans. David Farrell Krell (San Francisco: Harper, 1991), 1: 157–58.

41. Heidegger, *Being and Time*, p. 152.

42. Ibid., p. 154.

43. Heidegger, *Beiträge zur Philosophie*, p. 319.

44. Ibid., p. 444.

45. For a development of this point in reaction against the view of Heidegger as a "subjective solipsist," see Robert Bernasconi, "'The Double Concept of Philosophy' and the Place of Ethics in *Being and Time*," in *Heidegger in Question* (Atlantic Highlands, N.J.: Humanities Press, 1993).

46. Hans Jonas, "Heidegger's Resoluteness and Resolve," in Neske and Kettering, *Martin Heidegger and National Socialism*, p. 202.

47. See, e.g., Franz Neumann, *Behemoth* (New York: Oxford University Press, 1944), and Hans Sluga (who agrees with Neumann on this point), *Heidegger's Crisis*, p. 192. Even if the latter claim were true, of course, it would not mean that *Heidegger's* Nazism was not coherent or that it was unrelated to "the rest" of his philosophical system (as Sluga goes on to conclude).

48. Karsten Harries, "Heidegger as a Political Thinker," in *Heidegger and Modern Philosophy*, ed. Michael Murray (New Haven: Yale University Press, 1978), p. 312.

49. Sluga, for example, posits a condition of "necessary" connection if a substantive relation is to be credited between Heidegger's political expression and his "philosophical" views. Since that condition is not met, Sluga concludes that the origin of Heidegger's political view must be sought elsewhere (specifically, for him, in the cultural context; see, e.g., pp. 8 ff.). But it seems clear that one could acknowledge such cultural influence without denying that the causal connection between his metaphysics and his political views might be probable or dispositional, not deductive.

50. Heidegger, *Beiträge zur Philosophie*, pp. 42–43.

51. Jürgen Habermas, "Work and Weltanschauung: The Heidegger Controversy from a German Perspective," in *The New Conservatism*, trans. Sherry Weber Nicholson (Cambridge: MIT Press, 1989), pp. 148, 159.

52. Richard Bernstein, "Heidegger's Silence? Ethos and Technology," in *The New Constellation* (Cambridge: MIT Press, 1992), pp. 133–34.

53. Michael E. Zimmerman, "The Thorn in Heidegger's Side: The Question of National Socialism," *Philosophical Forum* 20 (1989): 341.

54. See Wolin, *Heidegger Controversy*, p. 163.

NOTES TO CHAPTER FOUR

1. For an account of Marr's views and his founding of the "Anti-semiten-Liga" ("League of Antisemites"), see Moshe Zimmerman, *Wilhelm Marr* (New York: Oxford University Press, 1986), chap. 7; P. G. J. Pulzer, *The Rise of Political Anti-Semitism in Germany and Austria* (New York: Wiley, 1964), pp. 47–52.

2. See, for example, Nathan Rotenstreich, *The Recurring Pattern: Studies in Anti-Judaism* (London: Weidenfeld and Nicolson, 1963).

3. Cf. Zimmerman, *Wilhelm Marr*, pp. 114–15.

4. Harold Nicolson, *Diaries* (New York: Atheneum, 1966–68), entry for 18 June 1945.

5. Immanuel Kant, *Anthropologie*, part 1, section 46.

6. This is the basis as well for the verdict of some commentators who reject the charge of antisemitism against Heidegger: e.g., Philippe Lacoue-Labarth, *Heidegger, Art, and Politics*, trans. Chris Turner (Oxford: Basil Blackwell, 1990), pp. 28–29; Heinrich Wiegand Petzet, *Encounters and Dialogues with Martin Heidegger, 1929–1976*, trans. Parvis Emad and Kenneth Maly (Chicago: University of Chicago Press, 1993), p. 29.

7. Heidegger, *Being and Time*, p. 121.

8. See Rainer Martin, "Heidegger and the Greeks," in *The Heidegger Case: On Philosophy and Politics*, ed. Tom Rockmore and Joseph Margolis (Philadelphia: Temple University Press, 1992), pp. 173–74.

9. Stephen Jay Gould, *Ever since Darwin* (New York: Norton, 1977), p. 231.

10. In fact the *criteria* for Jewish identity were not defined and announced until 14 November, but the rush toward the laws themselves had the effect mentioned. See Raul Hilberg, *The Destruction of the European Jews* (New York: Holmes and Meier, 1985).

11. See, e.g., Naomi Zack, *Race and Mixed Race* (Philadelphia: Temple University Press, 1993). The principle of racial definition in the United States, to the effect that *any* black ancestry, irrespective of the number of intervening generations, justifies categorizing the person as black (but that

the same criterion does not hold for white "blood"), epitomizes the tendentiousness of the category of race itself.

12. A version of this defense appears in Ernst Nolte's book on Heidegger (*Martin Heidegger: Politik und Geschichte im Leben und Denken* [Berlin: Propylaen, 1992]), where Nolte argues that a *real* antisemite "opposes Jews and tries to get rid of them *as* Jews with no exceptions allowed" (pp. 29–30). Thus Heidegger "was the exact opposite of Adolf Hitler, and such he would have remained even if he occasionally said that he had no sympathy for Jews or that the Jews in America were working against him" (pp. 290–91). On the condition that Nolte sets, *most* even self-professed antisemites would not "qualify"; some other term would be required, furthermore, for the lengthy pre-Nazi history of the persecution of the Jews that did not intend their physical extermination.

13. This is not to deny substantial differences among earlier moments in the history of antisemitism. But even if the extent to which "modern" antisemitism *derives* from its earlier counterparts remains an "open question," as Hannah Arendt claims in *The Origins of Totalitarianism* (San Diego: Harcourt Brace Jovanovich, 1985), p. vii, there can be little question about both the substantive and the functional resemblance between them.

14. See Berel Lang, "The Language of Genocide," in *Act and Idea in the Nazi Genocide*.

15. Heidegger, *Nietzsche*, 2:309.

16. See Martin Heidegger, *Schelling: Vom Wesen der menschlichen Freiheit* (Frankfurt am Main: Klostermann, 1982), pp. 40–41.

17. Dieter Thoma, "Making off with an Exile—Heidegger and the Jews," *New German Critique* 58 (1993): 79–85. In a context where genocide is being committed (or for that matter even threatened), this seems to me a distinction without a difference.

18. In arguably the most significant of these relationships, Heidegger and Hannah Arendt comment little in their writings meant for publication (he not at all, she only allusively) about any implications Heidegger's political stance has for that relationship. (Arendt refers to Heidegger's Nazi associations in her tribute to him on his eightieth birthday as a "professional deformation," evidently distinguishing it from both his professional accomplishments and any "personal" deformation.) See on this chap. 2, footnote 20 above.

19. See, for example, Max Müller, "Martin Heidegger: A Philosopher and Politics," in Neske and Kettering, *Martin Heidegger and National Socialism*, pp. 175–95.

20. Speech at Poznan, 4 October 1943, in *Documents on the Holocaust* (Jerusalem: Yad Vashem, 1981), p. 344.

21. Cited in Farias, *Heidegger and Nazism*, p. 210.

22. Cited in Ulrich Sieg, "Die Verjudung des deutschen Geistes," *Die Zeit*, 22 December 1989, p. 50. Tom Rockmore repeats Sieg's own claim that Heidegger's antisemitism is "established" by this one statement, in Tom Rockmore and Joseph Margolis, *The Heidegger Case* (Philadelphia: Temple University Press, 1992), p. 402. If a single assertion could justify that conclusion, this might do it—but a question remains whether, beyond any single statement, a *pattern* is required. (Nolte improbably claims that in this context *Verjudung* is "something like" a metaphor for "internationalization"—and so, presumably, harmless; Nolte, *Martin Heidegger*, p. 145.) In any event, I have attempted to show that the one statement does not have to stand by itself. (The same question can be raised in the other direction. So, for example, Walter Jens claims that Heidegger's retention of his tribute to Husserl in the text of *Being and Time* even when he dropped the book's dedication to Husserl in the 1943 edition "acquits" him (Neske and Kettering, *Martin Heidegger and National Socialism*, p. 225). But this conclusion is obviously debatable.

23. Toni Cassirer, *Aus meinem Leben mit Ernst Cassirer* (New York: privately published, 1950), p. 165.

24. Cited in Ott, *Martin Heidegger*.

25. Petzet, *Encounters and Dialogues with Martin Heidegger*, p. 40.

26. See "Ein Gespräch mit Max Müller," in *Martin Heidegger und das "Dritte Reich,"* ed. Bernd Martin (Darmstadt: Wissenschaftliche Buchgesellschaft, 1989).

27. Cited in Farias, *Heidegger and Nazism*, p. 121.

28. Ott, *Martin Heidegger*, p. 189.

29. Reprinted in Schneeberger, *Nachlese zu Heidegger*, p. 202. For a defense of Heidegger's claim of Heraclitean overtones, see Parvis Emad's introduction to Petzet, *Encounters and Dialogues with Martin Heidegger*, p. xxi. Emad agrees that Heidegger's "Nazi audience" would have understood something quite different from what he intended—but he sees this as no problem either for accurately interpreting Heidegger's words or for assessing his true intentions.

30. Blanchot, "Thinking the Apocalypse," p. 478.

31. See, e.g., Richard Evans, *Rethinking German History: Nineteenth Century Germany and the Origin of the Third Reich* (Boston: Allen and Unwin, 1987).

32. Pertinent examples here are too plentiful to warrant reference, although one notably mordant example appears in a statement by Yale University president James R. Angell, written *in early 1933*, to the Yale dean of admissions. The dean had been pleased to report to Angell his success in reducing the number of Jewish students admitted to Yale College, although conceding a still disproportionate (*sic*) number of admissions from Yale's home state of Connecticut. Angell responds: "I am extremely [inter-

ested] in the Hebraic record which you are kind enough to send me. The oscillations from year to year are rather larger than I would have expected. In any case, the material is very informing and it seems quite clear that, if we could have an Armenian massacre confined to the New Haven district, with occasional incursions into Bridgeport and Hartford, we might protect our Nordic stock almost completely" (cited in Dan A. Oren, *Joining the Club: A History of Jews and Yale* [New Haven: Yale University Press, 1985], pp. 62–63).

33. See Hannah Tillich, *From Time to Time* (New York: Stein and Day, 1973), p. 155.

34. Karl Löwith, "My Last Meeting with Heidegger, Rome, 1936," in Wolin, *Heidegger Controversy*, p. 142. A similar comment in which Heidegger defends himself on the grounds that he hoped to "stem the coming development by means of constructive powers which were still viable" appears in the *Spiegel* interview (Wolin, p. 92).

35. Marion Kaplan, "Anti-Semitism in Post-war Germany," *New German Critique* 58 (1993): 101.

36. Farias's discussion (*Heidegger and Nazism*, chap. 3) of the antisemitic currents that were part of Heidegger's earlier student days (at least as early as 1910), however circumstantial and inconclusive by itself, nonetheless becomes relevant when joined to the more explicit later evidence.

37. In addressing this issue, Babette Babich characterizes Heidegger's antisemitism as his "affective Nazism"—which seems to me to give too much (causal) weight to his antisemitism and too little to the more substantive philosophical grounds of his Nazism (Babette E. Babich, "The Ethical Alpha and the Linguistic Omega: Heidegger's Anti-Semitism and the Inner Affinity between Germany and Greece," *Joyful Wisdom* 1 [1994]: 3–25).

38. Richard Rorty, "Taking Philosophy Seriously," *New Republic*, 11 April 1988, p. 33. Rorty elsewhere proclaims an end to philosophy (as it has been), but his biological analogy here seems to represent philosophy as a natural, and so presumably constant, human disposition. See also on Heidegger's "accidental" Nazism, Richard Rorty, "Philosophy as Science, as Metaphor, and as Politics," in *Essays on Heidegger and Others* (Cambridge: Cambridge University Press, 1991).

39. See, e.g., Gregory S. Kavka, *Hobbesian Moral and Political Theory* (Princeton: Princeton University Press, 1986), and Henry M. Rosenthal, *The Consolations of Philosophy: Hobbes's Secret; Spinoza's Way* (Philadelphia: Temple University Press, 1989).

40. Joseph J. Kockelmans, *On the Truth of Being: Reflections on Heidegger's Later Philosophy* (Bloomington: Indiana University Press, 1984), pp. 264–65.

41. See, e.g., Sluga, *Heidegger's Crisis*, p. 99.

1. Rorty, "Taking Philosophy Seriously," p. 33.

2. See Robert Bernasconi, "Habermas and Arendt on the Philosopher's 'Error': Tracking the Diabolical in Heidegger," *Graduate Faculty Philosophy Journal*, 14/15 (1991), p. 4.

3. See, for example, Ettinger, *Hannah Arendt/Martin Heidegger*.

4. Theodor Adorno, Letter to *Diskus* (University of Frankfurt student newspaper), January 1963.

5. Jacques Derrida, "Philosopher's Hell: An Interview," in *The Heidegger Controversy*, ed. Richard Wolin (New York: Columbia University Press, 1991), p. 266.

6. I think here not only of such tendentiously negative accounts as Tony Judt's *Past Imperfect: French Intellectuals, 1944–1956* (Berkeley: University of California Press, 1992), but of tendentiously positive accounts like Simone de Beauvoir's *Adieux: A Farewell to Sartre*, trans. Patrick O'Brien (New York: Pantheon, 1984).

7. Lyotard, *Heidegger and "the jews,"* p. 52.

8. Jürgen Busche, "Also gut: Heidegger war ein Nazi!" in *Die Heidegger Controverse*, ed. Jürg Altwegg, (Frankfurt am Main: Athenäum, 1988), p. 184.

9. See, e.g., V. E. Conley, ed., *Rethinking Technologies* (Minneapolis: University of Minnesota Press, 1993); for a more nuanced view, see Michael Zimmerman, *Heidegger's Confrontation with Modernity: Technology, Politics, Art* (Bloomington: Indiana University Press, 1990), and see also Dana R. Villa, *Arendt and Heidegger: The Fate of the Political* (Princeton: Princeton University Press, 1995), 253–67.

NOTES TO THE APPENDIX

1. My initial diary entry: "At first meeting, in Heidegger's lecture in 1914, H. talked theology ('every other word was "Gott"'); he was a military censor at the time. When B. was first invited to H.'s house, by H.'s fiancée, H. after dinner read out loud from Dilthey for 2 hours." It seems hard to credit this date, since Baumgarten would have been just sixteen in 1914.

2. Gundolf was a prominent member of the George circle.

INDEX

Ford, Henry, 2, 113n1
Fränkel, Eduard, 36, 70, 108
Frege, Gottlob, 87

Gadamer, Hans-Georg, 86–87, 96
George, Stefan, 105, 125n2
Goebbels, Joseph, 62
Gould, Stephen Jay, 66, 121n9
Gundolf, Friedrich, 105, 125n

Habermas, Jürgen, 54–55, 114n4,
    121n51
Harries, Karsten, 53, 120n48
Hegel, G. W. F., 45
Heidegger, Hermann, 22
Heidegger, Martin, on Greece and
    Greek language, 3, 44, 55; on
    Nazism, 19–30, 38–39, 58, 72, 77,
    96; and postmodernism, 84–85;
    Rectoral Address, 24–25, 27, 45–46,
    53, 74–75; *Spiegel* interview, 22–24,
    44, 47; and technology, 16–18, 20,
    98, 125n9; "Volk" concept of, 8–9,
    26, 40–57
Heraclitus, 74–75
Herder, J. G., 98
Herzl, Theodor, 2, 113n1
Himmrich, 69
Hitler, Adolf, 63, 110–11, 119n31; and
    Mein Kampf, 74–75
Hobbes, Thomas, 81
Holocaust, 3–4, 14; and Heidegger,
    6–9, 16–19, 113n2; revisionism, 14, 18
Husserl, Edmund, 24, 71, 104, 106–8,
    116n16, 123n22

Israel, state of, 2–3

Jaspers, Karl, 24, 38, 72, 104, 108–9,
    118n8
Jens, Walter, 123n22
Jewish Question, as concept, 1–4,
    31–33
Jonas, Hans, 52–53, 120n46
Judt, Tony, 125n6

Kant, Immanuel, 63, 98, 97, 106–7,
    121n5

Katz, Jacob, 117n1
Kockelmans, Joseph J., 81, 124n40
Koenig, Pierre, 108
Krieck, Ernst, 37

Lang, Berel, 113n2, 115n4, 122n14
Lazare, Bernard, 2
Lenin, V. I., 2, 113n1
Lévinas, Emmanuel, 96
Löwith, Karl, 38, 76–77, 84, 124n34
Luban, David, 36, 71, 83, 101, 116n8,
    118n4
Lueger, Karl, 67
Lyotard, Jean-François, 95, 114n5,
    125n7

Mannheim, Karl, 103
Marcuse, Herbert, 21–22, 29, 58, 96,
    107, 116n17
Markowitz, Charles, 88
Marr, Wilhelm, 62–63, 121nn1, 3
Marx, Karl, 1, 48, 87, 113n1
Merleau-Ponty, Maurice, 96
Möllendorf, Wilhelm von, 104–5
Müller, Max, 72, 122n19

Nicolson, Harold, 63, 121n4
Nietzsche, Friedrich, 21, 47, 51, 68, 97
Nolte, Ernst, 116n9, 122n12
Nuremberg Laws, 66

Ott, Hugo, 74, 115n1, 116nn14, 15, 16;
    120n39, 123nn24, 28

Petzet, Heinrich Wiegand, 71, 121n6,
    123nn25, 29
Philosophy, in relation to biography,
    79–80, 87–92; in relation to politics,
    4–5, 15, 40, 42–43, 80–83, 85–92; as
    systematically non-deductive,
    80–82
Plato, x, 46, 93, 97, 98
Pound, Ezra, 76

Racism, biological vs. metaphysical,
    39, 65–68; and Heidegger, 25–27,
    64–68, 98
Rassinier, Paul, 14, 115n3

Renaut, Alain, 90, 114n6
Rockmore, Tom, 90, 117nn20, 23, 123n22
Rorty, Richard, 80, 86, 88, 124n38, 125n1
Rosenberg, Alfred, 25, 27
Rostovzeff, M. I., 103
Rousseau, Jean-Jacques, 87
Ryle, Gilbert, 86–87, 91, 95

Sartre, Jean-Paul, 2, 94, 96, 113n1
Schapiro, Meyer, 46
Schopenhauer, Arthur, 2
Schwörer, Victor, 70
Sluga, Hans, 46, 81, 118n6, 119n31, 120nn47, 49
Socrates, 47
Strauss, Leo, 27, 117n22
Sukale, Michael, 102, 109

Szilasi, Wilhelm, 103

Thoma, Dieter, 68, 122n17
Tillich, Hannah, 124n33
Tillich, Paul, 76
Tolstoy, Leo, 2, 113n1

Weber, Alfred, 105
Weber, Marianne, 105, 108
Weber, Max, 105, 107, 110
Weiss, Helene, 23–24, 106
Whitehead, Alfred North, 45, 119n29
Whitman, Walt, 91
Wisser, Richard, 116n13
Wittgenstein, Ludwig, 94

Zarader, Marlene, 117n3
Zimmerman, Michael, 56, 90, 121nn53, 3; 125n9